FINDING
TRUE LOVE

If you enjoyed *Finding True Love*, consider one or more of the following books by Daphne Rose Kingma from Conari Press:

A Garland of Love
Daily Reflections on the Magic and Meaning of Love

Heart & Soul
Living the Joy, Truth & Beauty of Your Intimate Relationship

A Lifetime of Love
How to Bring More Depth, Meaning and
Intimacy into Your Relationship

The Men We Never Knew
How to Deepen Your Relationship with the Man You Love

Coming Apart
Why Relationships End and How to Live through the Ending of Yours

The 9 Types of Lovers
Why We Love the People We Do and How They Drive Us Crazy

To Have and To Hold
A Wedding Keepsake

True Love
How to Make Your Relationship Sweeter,
Deeper and More Passionate

Weddings from the Heart
Contemporary and Traditional Ceremonies
for an Unforgettable Wedding

The Book of Love

Look for them in your local bookstore, on the Internet at
www.conari.com, or call Conari Press: 1-800-685-9595.

FINDING TRUE LOVE

The Four Essential Keys to Discovering the Love of Your Life

DAPHNE ROSE KINGMA

CONARI PRESS
Berkeley, California

🝗

Conari Press books are distributed by Publishers Group West

ISBN: 1-57324-564-X

Cover Design: Ame Beanland
Cover Photo: © Yuri Dojc/Image Bank

Library of Congress Cataloging-in-Publication Data
Kingma, Daphne Rose.
Finding true love : the four essential keys to discovering
the love of your life / Daphne Rose Kingma.
p. cm.
ISBN 1-57324-564-X (PB)
ISBN 1-57324-058-3 (HC)

1. Love.   2. Man–woman relationships.
3. Intimacy (Psychology)   I. Title.
HQ801.K556   1996
158'.2—dc20   96-14793

Printed in the United States of America.
01 02 03 04 05 RRD (NW) 10 9 8 7 6 5 4 3 2 1

For Esmé
who really needs to believe
that she can really fall in love

and

For Molly
who fell in love so beautifully

Acknowledgments

This book would not have come into being without all the love in my life. My deep thanks to those who keep me always in the cradle of their care, Chris, Victor, Sunta, Wink, Mary Jane, and Don.

Special thanks also to Kerry, who keeps me strong in spite of my aversion to the C-word, to Mary Ann Stephenson who follows (and holds) the flashlight, and to F.X. Feeney, for being there, still.

My loving thanks also to Kym Rousseau, for shiny assistance and happy encouragement, and to Laura Madsen, for being such an intelligent and joyful accomplice.

I am always grateful to the fine people at Conari Press, especially to Will Glennon for opening and smoothing my path, and to Mary Jane Ryan for the beauty of her indefatigability. Warm thanks also to Emily for elegant diplomacy, Erin for bright energy and kindness, Suzanne for integrity, Brenda for knowing intuition, Jennifer for laughter, Claudia for gentleness, Ame for exquisiteness, and Laura for sweet blessings. This web of care would not be complete without the fine male energies of David, Everton, Rally, and Tom. I thank you all; you grace my life.

Finally, and always, my deep thanks to Yvan for your courageous and abiding love.

Table of Contents

. . . .

The Path to Love . . . 1

*F*aith . . . 11

1. *Believe that Love Awaits You . . . 15*
2. *Make Yourself Available . . . 29*

*I*ntention . . . 45

3. *Know Your Real Self . . . 49*
4. *Discover Why Love Has Eluded You . . . 68*
5. *Develop Your Capacity for Love . . . 88*

*T*rust . . . 101

6. *Be Realistic About What Love Is . . . 105*
7. *Recognize the Higher Purpose of a Relationship . . . 124*
8. *Apprehend Your Soul's Wisdom in Creating a New Relationship . . . 137*

*S*urrender . . . 149

9. *Embrace the Paradox of Love . . . 153*
10. *Let Go of Preconceptions . . . 166*
11. *Leap into the Unknown . . . 184*
12. *Be Grateful . . . 196*

Love Readiness Inventory . . . 203
A Diagnostic Coda: Is This the One for Me? . . . 209

The Path to Love

*L*ove is an experience of great emotional and spiritual awakening to the unbounded bliss that is the true condition of our souls. When we fall in love, we feel no separation—between ourselves and the person we love or, for a time, from all others. It is the transcendent, luminous, lovely feeling of love that we desire most dearly, long for most passionately, and are filled by most deeply when it occurs in our lives. Love is a sanctuary for our spirits, a bath of empathy for our emotions, a tranquil meadow in which to nurture our fond hopes and dreams.

This book is a pathway to that love, a guide to the spiritual and emotional preparations you must make in order to attract love--love the magnificent, love the exquisite, love the sweet, kind, and consoling—into your life. For love doesn't come uninvited. The suitor, unconjured, will not arrive; the beloved, unlonged-for, refuses to make himself known. Love in the form of a person, a friend, a life partner in feeling and spirit, a body that comforts and thrills in ecstatic passion, must be asked for, consciously awaited, and intentionally invited in.

This book is meant to be an encouragement, an inspiration, and a directive to help you prepare your heart and soul for the arrival of the love of your life. It is an action book, because its premise is that you must take an active part in bringing love into your life, and that the universe will grant you love only to the extent that you are actually prepared for it. Learning the exact nature of what that action is is what this book is about.

Indeed, why you're still looking for love has to do with a lot of factors, both obvious and mysterious, that most of us usually don't account for. This book is an exploration of those factors so that, by expanding your awareness, you can stop being a person who is always somehow on the fringe, watching others fall in love, and move into the place of finding your own true love.

This exploration will take you on a journey of deep self-examination that will ask you to pause and really reflect on your life. At times you may wonder what all this self-reflection has to do with falling in love; at others you may see the connection clearly. But whether or not it's obvious at the moment, if you haven't yet found a person to love, this process can truly assist you. In fact, it is specifically designed to take you to the parts of yourself that hold the keys to finding love. So as you're going through the book, take time and take heart because each self-discovery, whether difficult or exciting, will bring love closer to you.

We often think that looking for love means answering personals ads, going to singles haunts, or joining dating services. These all have their place, but the most important aspects of our preparation for love are internal, and usually neglected. Real love, love that is deep and true and will last you a lifetime, will come to you not because of all these external behaviors, but because you have unfastened the psychological and spiritual locks that have prevented love from coming to you.

For, unbeknownst to most of us, it is these inner limitations, more than any external circumstances, that stand in our way when we're looking for love. That's why this book presents you with the four keys to true love: faith, intention, trust, and surrender.

Each of these four keys represents a spiritual attitude, which, as you incorporate it more and more, will serve to bring love toward you. Each key has a set of related steps that are the working out of that attitude. Some are psychological and will open the doors to your past and heal you from old wounds, some will get you in touch with your hope, others will acquaint you with your spiritual dimension, and still others will encourage you to become more realistic. As you read, incorporating the principles and doing the exercises, you will discover not only what you want love to bring to you, but also what you have to bring to it.

You may find these attitudes and behaviors oddly paradoxical, since they consist of both doing and not doing the very same things: trying harder *and* giving up, holding on *and* letting go. We don't often approach life this way, especially when we want a specific outcome. We tend to choose behaviors that fall on one side or the other. But the truth is that in the world of love, of spirit and emotion, things are always paradoxical. They operate apart from logic, good sense, cunning, or reason. They require a revision not only of our usual behaviors but also of many internal attitudes we hold without even knowing it.

Underpinning this book are certain assumptions I believe are always operating in the background of our quests for love. The first of these is that love is all around us. Like the air we breathe, it's the very condition in which we exist, and in this grand sea of love that surrounds us there is a person waiting to fall in love with you.

Awareness of the omnipresence of love is the essential condition of falling in love, which is a little like picking fruit from a tree. If you've ever walked into a cherry orchard when the trees were crimson with fruit, you know that all you have to do is reach up and open your hands, and the ripe fruit will fall into them. Love is like that—abundant, lush, just waiting for us to reach up and take it. But if you don't believe love is all around, you'll certainly never receive it.

The second assumption is that love is our true condition. Anything other than "being in love," the state of blissful connection to another, and ultimately to all other human beings, is an aberration to our souls. As souls, the only thing we recognize as worth doing is to love. We seek love in every form and on the most exalted and ordinary levels, because love is our one true undertaking.

The third assumption is that we each have the power to love. We all have the capacity to love and be loved. In some of us, that capacity is highly developed, radiant, and shining. In others, it's like an old piece of silver, an heirloom that needs to be polished and reclaimed. But because love is our soul's true destiny, each of us does contain a portion of this grand capacity to love. Whatever its measure—a crumb or an avalanche, a cipher or a great fortune—we all contain the spark of love that is waiting to be ignited.

In fact, this is the real nature of "falling in love." It isn't becoming something we're not or getting a prize we don't really deserve; rather, it is removing the layers of batting and resistance that have encumbered us, preventing us from revealing our true nature to ourselves.

Since we all have the power to love and love is our true life's work, it is our highest obligation to remove all our impediments to love. These impediments may be emotional, requiring you to heal from the wounds that are inevitably inflicted by the mere experience of being a person in a family; or they may be spiritual, in the form of not truly believing in union or not having had enough experience of deep connection to allow you to believe that love could ever be there for you. Finally, they may be circumstantial, as in being so involved in a particular lifestyle that love, even when it's standing right in front of you, can't possibly be recognized. Finding the love of your life, therefore, is a process of sloughing off, paring down, and peeling away all the encrustations that prevent you from fulfilling your heart's true longing.

Love—this great love that's all around you and wants to come to you in the form of a person—won't come to you unless you really focus on it. Great artists, writers, musicians, and entertainers, great spiritual masters and world leaders have attained their mastery not by dissipating their energies, but by eliminating distractions, holding a focus, and believing that the one thing their whole hearts desired would truly come to them. The same is true for you. That's why this book is designed, above all, to help you define and refine your focus.

Finally, as you begin, I ask you to enter this process holding the assumption that everything you've already been through in your life is the preparation for where you are now. All the dramas and traumas with your family, and all your past relationships, whether wonderful or difficult, have been preparing you for the relationship you are seeking now. If you hadn't experienced all that has already happened to you, you wouldn't be the person you are now, nor would you be able to receive love in the specific form in which it will arrive for you.

The same is true for the person who will show up to be the love of your life. He or she has also been on a long journey of preparation that will eventually lead to you. Viewed in this way, nothing either of you has done is a mistake or a waste of time; everything has served to ready you for the moment of your convergence. Remember—you are being prepared for someone who is also being prepared for you. And when you both arrive in the same place at the same time, that glorious moment will be the culmination of all your preparations.

This little book is here to help you make your preparation a conscious undertaking. I wish you an insightful and healing journey, and a wonderful love with whom to share the rest of your life.

one

Faith

. . . .

Believe in a love that is being stored up for
you like an inheritance, and have faith that
in this love there is a strength and a blessing
so large that you can travel as far as you
wish without having to step outside it.

—Rainer Maria Rilke

. . . .

Faith is belief in the unseen, the quietly held conviction that even though you can't imagine how, at some time, in some place, in the right way, the thing you desire will indeed come to pass. Faith is a spiritual attitude that allows you to live knowing that, in spite of whatever may be happening now, something completely different can happen; everything can change.

Faith is the way we know beyond reason, feel beyond logic, relax beyond our good sense. Faith is quiet and still. It doesn't go around trumpeting its expectations. It emerges in the gentle places of your inner being where all the sound, rush, and demands of life aren't clawing at you. Faith is the silence in the cathedral, the calm at the center of the storm where you can rest in the knowing that something new and beautiful will occur.

Faith is not invested in specific outcomes—that the thing you desire will arrive in a particular way, at exactly the time you would like it. It is the overriding conviction that your life is unfolding according to a plan that existed even before you were born.

At times, faith may seem like a wispy, optimistic attitude held foolishly against all odds. In fact, faith is strength of the spirit expressing itself in the world. Faith is about recognizing that you are a spirit, an eternal being whose existence began before this lifetime and will continue after this life is over. Faith knows that what it knows is true, no matter what the world or your own doubts might say to the contrary.

It's faith talking when the parents of a terminally ill child say, "We knew the experimental procedure would work, even though odds were 10,000 to 1." Faith says such things as: Everything happens for a reason; whatever you need will come to you; miracles do happen; I *will* find the person of my dreams.

None of these statements is as obviously strong as the steel girders that hold up the freeway overpass, but these are the things faith recognizes to be true. Faith knows in its surety that what you believe, more than anything else, will truly affect your life, change how you feel, and bring you to your true destination.

Faith in love is knowing that there's a grand design for your life and that everything will work out, even if you don't know exactly how. It's understanding that the surprises will be more satisfying than what you've already planned on, and that love is the greatest power and most delicious experience in the world. It is the bliss of trusting that everything will be perfectly given, and that you really will find a person to love.

1. *Believe that Love Awaits You*

If you've been sitting around for years in your cubby hole in the singles apartment, watching the handsome guy at the pool who never looks up to see you staring out the window, if you've been overwhelmed by a career that hasn't left time for intimacy, if all your friends are married and you feel like the only person in the world who hasn't found "the one," then you may well be in the state of believing that there's never going to be a true love for you.

If that's the case, then this is exactly when you need to start believing that love does indeed await you. Nobody falls in love without, somewhere deep inside, believing that a wonderful love is possible for them. Just as nobody gets to Paris without believing that Paris exists, falling in love is something you have to imagine and believe in.

That's because conceptualization creates reality. In the story of almost every successful tycoon, we read that there was a belief against all odds that he or she would succeed some day, a vision of a future that was completely invisible in the present. It's no different with any of us: what becomes manifest in our lives arrives because consciously and unconsciously, we believe it can happen—whether it's a better job, a new car, or a true love. When it comes to love, it's as if there's a great supermarket in the sky saying, "We'd be happy to order up this special person for you. We don't ordinarily carry men and women but if you'll just ask, we'd be more than happy to send out the one that's perfect for you."

So it is that the precondition of love's ever arriving is that you believe that somewhere out there is a real live person for you to love. If you believe it, it'll be true; if you don't, it will never happen. In fact, the person who could be the love of your life could step right up and look you in the eye, and you could say, excuse me, and head off post-haste in exactly the opposite direction.

Believing that there's a true love for you may seem like a very small thing, but for a lot of us there's a great hovering doubt that this wonderful thing called love could actually happen to us. Maybe you've already had twenty-four lousy relationships, maybe your fiance died in a car crash, maybe you've always believed you aren't pretty enough, smart enough, or successful enough, or you're so shy that you can't even imagine having the kind of conversation that could get you into a relationship in the first place.

Remember Cinderella? She lay in rags on her pile of cinders and dusted up after her nasty stepmother and step-sisters. The furthermost thing from her mind was that she, the raggedy cinder-sweeper, could ever fall in love.

But deep inside, Cinderella had faith, because when the Fairy Godmother showed up, she was totally open to what occurred. She was open on a very deep level to the possibility that something good could happen to her, be-cause when it presented itself, she didn't run away. We might even go so far as to say that it was her faith, her own inner conviction, that *created* the Fairy Godmother with the magic wand, the pumpkin, the exquisite glass slippers, and even the Prince.

All these were manifestations of the possibility of love that somehow, in her heart of hearts, she had already believed in. She put her faith in the Fairy Godmother, she accepted that the pumpkin turned into a coach, and she stepped into the little glass slippers with absolute confidence. She didn't say, "My goodness, how do you expect me to walk on these, they're going to splinter the minute I put my feet inside them?" No, she was open to it because deep inside, she'd already said, "I believe miracles can happen, and if one does, I'm going to rise to the occasion and allow the magic to be bestowed upon me."

If you don't believe in Fairy Godmothers, you'll certainly never see one. And if you don't believe in love, it will never show up for you either.

So it is that the first step you need to take is to open your heart and believe there is a person for you. He or she is like a beautiful bird circling the planet, waiting for the invitation to alight in your garden and say, "Here I am. I heard your call. I've been flying around waiting for the moment when you would invite me to sit in your tree, to enchant you with my song, to make your heart sing."

A Twofold Undertaking

Believing in love is a twofold undertaking. It requires, first of all, that you believe there is such an energy as love in the world, and secondly that you believe that love in the form of a particular person will also be available to you. Love is a vast energy that's around us all the time. It's just looking for a way to be embodied in human form. But if you don't believe this energy exists, you'll certainly never experience your particular cupful of it. It will only be an idea.

On the other hand, if you begin to say to yourself, "I know love is out there; I know it's the greatest power in the world, and I want my share of it," then a very beautiful thing will start to happen. You will start to encounter love on every corner, in the eyes of every person you meet, in poignant moments you share with strangers, in the sweetness you share with your friends. And if you ask for it specifically and believe that it will come, you will also experience it in the form of a particular person to fall happily in love with.

Believing that love awaits you is more than having a vague, odd, floating notion that somewhere out there love might exist. It means holding a powerful, beautifully honed, highly developed conviction that love is specifically available to you. The person of your dreams, the human being who is your excellent counterpart, the one who can actually nourish, excite, delight, and fulfill you, really does exist.

The difference between the kind of belief I'm talking about and the sort of passive, well-maybeish hope you might have is that you are actually convinced in your heart that this magical thing can happen to you. If what you want is a real live human being to love, you really must start believing that there is such a critter out there wandering around, and that he or she is in just as much of a state of longing as you are. Rather than saying "Well, maybe someday someone will come along," which, in the world of the spirit, is a kind of giving up, you must say, "I'm taking a stand that such a person exists and absolutely will show up in my life."

I remember many years ago talking to a woman who lived in the same apartment complex as I did when we both were young married women in Washington, D.C. One day, when we were having tea, she said, "I always used to be worried that I'd never fall in love and get married because I'm not pretty. But then, one day, I was in my mother's kitchen, and I looked at all her old kettles and pans, and I realized that for every crooked pot there was a crooked lid. So I stopped worrying about whether I was pretty enough, because I knew that there was someone out there who would be just right for me, a person whose imperfections would be the perfect complement to mine."

I can remember, as vividly as if it were yesterday, that just as she was finishing the story, her charming husband came home. Her belief, even in the face of what she knew to be her own limitations, was what allowed her to become available to love, and her availability is what allowed her husband to find her.

The same is true for you. For not only is there a crooked pot for every crooked lid, but there's also a king for every queen and a mirror for every face that chooses to look into it. There is a heart and a soul that is the counterpart to each heart and soul that is asking for love. So if you want to fall in love, believe in love, and surely it will come to you.

How Belief Works

Many of us receive things in life that appear to show up out of nowhere. We unexpectedly make a friendship. We get a new job on a minute's notice. We win a free vacation to a beautiful tropical island. We fall heir to an unexpected mini-fortune. What occurs may seem to have nothing to do with belief, but it only appears that way on the surface.

The other day the telephone repairman told me about how he and his wife had for years dreamt of leaving the desert and moving to a town by the ocean. One night he came home from work and told his wife that that very day he'd been offered a job in the town of their dreams. He'd had to decide on the spot, and he'd already signed up for the job.

Although she was a little anxious, his wife was also excited. This was their dream, after all, the thing they'd been wanting to do for years—but how were they going to do it? For six months, while his family stayed behind, the man commuted to his new job. At times both he and his wife got discouraged: The new town was expensive; they began to wonder if they'd ever be able to afford a house.

Then, one night, just before he started back to the desert to join his wife for the weekend, he pulled off the freeway to get some gas. As he travelled down a side road in the dark, he saw a wonderful old house with a For Sale sign in the front yard. He went up and knocked on the door, and, even though it was late, the owner, a charming old lady, invited him in. He loved the house, and she was so happy that a person who could really appreciate her house had arrived that she lowered the price and sold it to him that night. He and his wife still live there, he told me, and that's where his sons both spent a wonderful childhood.

This story of a couple who found their dream house in their dream town is an example of how everything comes to us in life. Somewhere in the back rooms of our consciousness, we've already asked for whatever arrives. This asking is faith, an expression of the quiet inner conviction that somewhere we already believe that the things we are seeking await us.

The importance of believing that love actually awaits you is that rather than being in a state of passivity—vaguely imagining that a special someone might come along (but you're afraid it'll never really happen)—you're in a state of invitation. People and miracles respond to invitations; whereas passivity—the form our doubts take—creates a block between us and whatever wants to come in. This state of passivity is sort of like saying, "If you beat your way to my door, maybe I'll let you come in, but don't expect a warm reception." On the other hand, believing love awaits you means that you are consciously saying, "I know there's someone out there, and I'm going to hold myself in a welcoming, receptive stance." Love wants to come into your life; it's just waiting for your engraved invitation, so start designing it now.

Conscious Wanting

The old woman who sold her house had a For Sale sign on it. That was the outward expression of her inward belief that she was ready to move. Similarly, the man and his wife believed, even in the difficult hours, that everything would turn out right, so they could move to the town of their dreams.

Like these dreamers, believing love awaits you means that you're putting every cell of your consciousness on-line for that belief. Consciously believing means that you will labor to set aside all the "what-if's," all the "oh but it can't be's," and all the "yeah, but it'll never happen to me's" that are so easy to fall into. Believing doesn't mean that you will never doubt again, because belief itself is a process with many steps on its path, but it does mean that your doubts will gradually start to recede.

That's because believing love awaits you means giving up again and again all the reasons you have for feeling that falling in love could never happen to you. It means that, against whatever years of frustrating and disappointing experiences you've already had, you continue to take a position of hope and try to hold it unflinchingly. In a larger sense, it means you recognize that the universe is kindly and benign, that it wants to bless you with love, that it senses your hunger and believes you're deserving.

The forging of this belief is one of the ways the spirit of love works with us to develop our belief. The love that is all around us, that is the very matrix of our existence, is constantly surrounding us with an atmosphere in which we can feel its pulsing beautiful presence. It's as if love itself is saying, "Come on, dive in; the ecstatic experience is real; it's here for you, too." Belief is the internal process that affirms this, that whispers, "Oh, maybe this *could* be true. I'll tiptoe into believing."

This is the first step down the path of belief. And when we take that little step, we're often rewarded with an experience that supports our belief and allows us to hold it a little more deeply: There's a blessing on some work we've done, a breakthrough in a difficult situation with a colleague, a surprise bouquet of flowers arrives, or a new friendship blossoms.

These are the circles of response to the pebbles we shyly toss in the pond of our conviction. They allow us to take a further step, to refine our belief, to say not only, "Maybe good things can happen," but also, "The love I need and desire will surely be there."

Patience on the Way

Because belief itself is a process, you need to be patient with yourself. On the journey to believing, there inevitably will be little hurts and disappointments, because the person you love isn't necessarily going to show up this afternoon at your front door. Along the way, there will be unsuitable suitors, the women who aren't the girl of your dreams, the man who's not Mister Right but just Mister Right-Now, the person who's not the love of your life but the love of your Club Med vacation.

All these times when someone arrives who isn't quite perfect aren't opportunities to give up. In fact, they're just the opposite, occasions in which you can say, "Oh, here's a tiny beginning. Now that I see that something is being created for me somewhere out there in the distance, I can deepen my belief that the love of my life really does exist."

These apparently wrong persons are little spiritual tests that show up along the way to strengthen your resolve. The temptation, of course, is to say, "He wasn't perfect, so that just goes to show there isn't any love out there." But don't give up. Instead, try to say, "Well, someone arrived, so I can begin to trust that at least I'm on the path."

These seeming missteps ought to be viewed not as failures of love, but as chances for you to sharpen and deepen your relationship skills and self-awareness. The truth is we get only the quality of love that we're prepared for. So use your disappointments—not only as opportunities to deepen your conviction about the possibility of love, but also as occasions to develop your capacity for love.

Concretizing Your Belief

Holding this belief is very important—that's why it's the first step in this book. But it's also important to concretize this belief in some way. What I mean by this is that there are things you can do, words you can say, or actions you can take that will make your belief visible to you on an ongoing basis. This is crucial, because when we manifest our convictions—through words and behaviors—we're more able to perceive that we're living in this state of positive expectation.

To do this, I suggest that you create a prayer, meditation, or ceremony that will remind you day by day that you are abiding in the state of believing that love awaits you. When you create a prayer, meditation, or ceremony, and actually utter the words that express your longing, you send out to the spirit of love the earnestness of your quest. The words you utter are half a dialogue asking for a response. They confirm not only the seriousness of your desire, but also your expectation of an answer.

To show how this might operate for you, let me tell you a story: A young man I worked with years ago in therapy stopped by to see me recently, with his lovely young bride at his side. During our work together he had concentrated on resolving painful childhood issues, particularly as they had inhibited his career. When he finally made a break-through in this area, he was offered a wonderful job in New York City. He left excited, but as he said his farewells, he expressed regret that he hadn't yet fallen in love. When he returned to share his good fortune, and I asked him where he'd met his wife, he said simply, "She found me—but I helped. I lured her with a ceremony.

"In each corner of my living room, I laid out an offer-ing for my love, what I hoped she would be attracted to—in one corner a pearl, in another the tape of some beautiful music, in another some lines from a poem that's always touched me deeply, in another a bottle of scented oil. Each morning after a time of quiet meditation, I said a prayer in each of the four directions—north, south, east and west—asking that my love be sent to me.

"I said my prayer every morning for two years, but no matter where I went, no matter who introduced me to their friends or how many blind dates I had, I never met a single woman who interested me. People thought I was crazy, and toward the end, I was beginning to wonder if I wasn't a little crazy myself. But I never gave up. Somehow, I always believed that she was out there somewhere.

"Then, one day, out of the blue, *she* showed up at my door—the door to my office, actually. She was applying for a job the next floor up, and had gotten off the elevator at the wrong floor. She came in to ask me directions, and the rest, as they say, is history."

Like our man in New York, you may use a prayer, meditation, offering, ceremony, or any combination of the four. Your prayer can be as simple as, "Please send me the love of my life," but it should be direct in its asking. That's because asking is, in itself, an expression of the faith that what you have asked for will be granted, and thus it brings forth the asked-for thing.

If you prefer, you can express your prayer in the form of an affirmation. For example, "The love I desire, the love that will bring me the greatest joy and fulfill my highest purpose, is already on its way to me."

You may want to extend your prayer into the form of a meditation, a series of words that have a rhythmic or poetic quality, that you can repeat to yourself throughout the day: "The love I need, the love I can receive, the love I long to give and share—I seek this precious love."

Finally, if you prefer, you can create a small ceremony for the invocation of love. Let your ritual be one of your own making; it must come from your heart and be an expression of how you feel and what you want. To give you some ideas, I suggest the following: Light a candle each morning and say a prayer. Or put a beautiful object by your door that symbolizes love to you. Touch it each day as you leave your house and say a little prayer for love. Or hang a mirror in your hallway and look into it once a day and say, "I'm looking for the love that is a reflection of myself."

Whatever you do, trust that your meditations and prayers are being heard. The answer may not come in just the way you expect: The young man's bride showed up at his office, not his apartment, but the faith he held did eventually bring the desired results. Believing that love awaits you is knowing that the love you are asking for is already being prepared for you and that, even if it hasn't arrived, it is already approaching.

2. Make Yourself Available

If you were ever a kid who walked up and down a street looking for a penny in the gutter, you know what it is to make yourself available to what appears to be impossible. People don't leave money on the street for us to gather up in our hot little hands, but if you're a determined child and you walk around the block enough times, chances are you'll find that shiny penny.

Being available to love is a lot like that. You have to present yourself at every opportunity and show up everywhere with every level of your being.

The How-to-Snag-a-Man type relationship books tell us that this showing up consists of buying a great wardrobe, going to singles bars, placing personals ads, and engaging in all kinds of wily, seductive, and ultimately self-erasing behaviors that might get you to cross paths with someone who's just as inauthentically pursuing you. All these methods do, of course, increase your statistical possibilities of meeting *someone*. If you utilize them often enough and with enough conviction, chances are you will run across somebody who will take you to the movies or even marry you.

But if you're reading *this* book, chances are not only that you've done such things with less than fabulous success, but also that you'd like to meet a real person, who could deeply love the real you. And that requires being truly available.

· · · · · · · ·

There's more to being available than having your body in a particular environment where somebody else's body might also simultaneously show up, or even your image on a video screen where somebody else's video self can be reviewed by you. There's more to availability than just having a hot outfit or being tall, dark, and handsome. In fact, there are a number of levels to availability, many of which are internal.

What we're really talking about is inner availability, a heart that is saying, "I'm ready, I'm willing, I'm curious; I'm putting myself on the line on every conceivable level, to allow love into my life."

This is very different and much more subtle than buying a new dress and showing up at the party. It means you've addressed your inhibitions (I'm scared or I'm shy) and prohibitions (I'm too old or I've failed at love too many times), and that despite all your reasonable fears, you've sent out the message, "Here I am, Love, come get me; I'm yours."

What does it take internally to be able to actually utter these peppermint-candy-heart kind of statements? It takes being open.

Being open refers to the way we approach the world, our circumstances, other human beings, and the experience of being alive itself. We have two choices. We can participate in life as if it were an insult or an assault, something we have to put up with and constantly fight against, or we can be here as receptive human beings who say, "I know there's something purposeful and beautiful here, and I'm open to discover what it is. I'm just one person, bumbling along on my life's little path, but I'm certainly willing to be surprised."

Being open is the stance of vulnerability, welcoming the unexpected, being available to the mysterious, being curious about the strange and the mundane, and being willing to entertain the unexpected in every dimension.

Developing Openheartedness

If we want love to enter our lives, we need to be open in a variety of ways. It isn't enough to be intellectually open, to say, "Well, I think love's a great idea, and if someone showed up, I'd certainly give some thought to falling in love." We need to be open with our hearts as well, and with our feelings and our attitudes.

To be open with your heart means that you have consciously acknowledged that no matter what wounds you've already suffered (and we've all suffered more than it feels like we can bear), you're still willing to be open to love. It's like there's a little voice inside you saying, "I know my heart's been broken 50,000 times, but I still want the butterfly of love to fly down and sit on my shoulder. Besides, my broken heart is so strong from breaking all those times that it will just jump for joy when my true love arrives."

Being emotionally open isn't an easy place to come to.

It's not a state that just descends on you without any effort on your part. It takes work. It means that somewhere along the way you've faced head on (and worked through) the fact that your heart *has* been broken, that you're tremendously vulnerable, that you do have doubts and fears, and that despite your fears, you're willing to try again.

In a larger sense, being openhearted indicates that you recognize yourself as an emotional being, and are willing to go through the experience of your feelings. You realize that your emotions—joy, sorrow, fear, and anger—are the constant undercurrent that moves through your body, and you are willing to feel them.

We all have a constant flow of feelings, and whether or not we're willing to experience them is what makes us open like flowers or closed like tombs. Letting your feelings move through you keeps you emotionally flexible, up-to-date. Because you're not bringing a catalog of fears, anger, and resentments from the past, your heart is in a state of openness. Then, when you meet someone who might be appropriate for you, you can bring yourself wholeheartedly to the experience.

To see how you're doing in this department, ask yourself the following questions:

- Do I have a positive, curious, welcoming, trusting attitude about most human beings?

- Would I be willing to work through the wounds of my childhood to open my heart to another person?

- Would I be willing to give up my memories of the heart-break in my previous relationships to love again?

If not, make a pledge to yourself that you will ask each day for the resolution of these hurts. When you consciously ask for this healing, it will be forthcoming.

Come Out of Your Cave

Being available may also require a change of behavior. For example, rather than hiding out, staying home every Friday night, putting your cold cream on and wishing you had a date, you might make yourself available by accepting an invitation to a party. But true availability goes way beyond just showing up. When you're at the party, all of you needs to be available: your words, your personality, and your spirit. That means that you make conversation even if you're shy, speak even if you're not spoken to, express appreciation, admiration, curiosity. If someone inquires about who you are, why you're there, or what you want out of life, you cough up the truth—"I'm here because I've been hiding out for fifteen years and now I want to find a relationship"—and not just some coy party jargon.

Making yourself available means that instead of being down in the dumps about your chances at love, you become ridiculously optimistic. Along these lines, I've always enjoyed the old joke in which an old man stands on the corner day after day and every time a beautiful woman walks by he yells out to her, "Hey, would you come over here and give me a kiss?" Most women would walk right by looking insulted. Sometimes, a woman would smile sort of pityingly, and every once in a dozen blue moons, a woman would actually come over and give the old man a kiss.

Finally, a shopkeeper on the corner who had watched all this for several weeks came over and said, "Don't you realize what a stupid fool you look like asking all these women if they'd like to kiss you?" And the old man replied, "Well maybe that's true, but I'll bet I've had more beautiful women kiss me than you ever have."

In his rather unconventional way, this man was making himself available. He was saying, "I'm standing out here on the corner, not just watching all the girls go by, but being willing to take the risk of asking for what I really want. The odds are against it, but, by golly, every once in a while it actually happens."

As our man on the street demonstrates, if you have an optimistic attitude and make yourself available, your chances of getting what you want are immediately increased. Being available runs the gamut from going on the Sierra Club hike, even though you're falling-over exhausted after a 90-hour work week, to the spiritual brazenness of getting down on your hands and knees, shaking your fists at God and saying, "Send me someone right now, because I can't stand being alone for one more minute."

If you're staying home watching TV every night, you're never going to meet anybody except the TV repairperson. That's why, as the dating manuals have always taught us, you *should* put yourself in circumstances where people congregate- church, the Arthur Murray studio, your best friend's cousin's wedding reception; You *should* go on all the blind dates that everybody you know sets up for you; you *should* join the computer dating service and even write the catchy, truthful, vulnerable personals ad that will capture some fine someone's attention.

All these things are worth doing—I know at least one beautiful marriage that has resulted from each of these techniques. But there's also another kind of availability that's about "staying in here" rather than "going out there." This availability starts where you already are, and has to do with turning your immediate environment into a kind of invitation.

Feather Your Nest

Just as sitting at home watching TV and eating corn chips can be your resistance to a relationship—you're behaving as if there's only ever going to be you to love you—so a new attitude about your personal environment can turn it from a hiding place into the very circumstance that can bring a relationship toward you.

I call this "feathering your nest." It refers to creating an environment which is itself so enticing that it announces to you at every turn that you and it are available for someone to come and share. I have a friend who, when her last relationship ended, stripped off the bed sheets, burned them in a ceremonial fire, then went downtown to buy a gorgeous new set of sheets. Even though she knew she wasn't yet ready for a new relationship, it was her way of saying, "I'm preparing for a new person to share my bed and my life. I don't know when he'll show up, but I'm anticipating his arrival and preparing a welcome for him."

When you consciously take the actions of invitation—whether that's redecorating your living room, getting a great new haircut, refurbishing your wardrobe, building the house you hope the woman of your dreams would adore—you increase your chances of finding love. That's not because these are all effective seduction traps, but because they're the way you're sending out your S.O.S. to the invisible forces: "I'm here with my haircut," "I'm here with my bedsheets, "I'm here with my house; I'm ready, please answer my plea."

Like prayers and ceremonies, all these nest-feathering behaviors are actually faith in action, the outward manifestation of your belief. We need to take as many of these actions of faith as possible. That's because we never know which of our behaviors is going to bring the results. We're *participants* in the process, not in charge of it, because love is always a gift. But we still have to put forth *all* efforts, leave no stone unturned, and above all, keep the faith until we can see who the cosmos is choosing for us.

This reminds me of an old movie, *Three Coins in the Fountain,* in which three American girls, traveling in Rome, each toss a coin into the beautiful Fountain of Trevi. The legend is that if you make a wish as you throw your coin in the fountain, your wish will be granted. In true Hollywood style, each girl's wish did get fulfilled, but not exactly as she imagined—in an even more wonderful way.

In a sense, in our search for love, we're all like these travelers to Rome, tossing our coins in, making our wishes, waiting for magic. Availability consists of a variety of actions, both inner and outer. Once you really decide to make yourself available, and you translate your availability into concrete behaviors—speaking to one new person each time you go to the gym, for example, or asking every woman you've been even mildly attracted to out to lunch—you start becoming *really* available; you're on-line for a love miracle to happen.

The reason this ultimately achieves results is that you're also telling *yourself* that you're available. You're acting out your availability in circumstances that will mirror it back to you, and since, at heart, we're all very simple souls, we need to have a concrete demonstration of what we're feeling. We need our inner states to be outwardly expressed—especially to ourselves. That's why taking action is so important. It provides external reminders; it shows us what we're up to.

Just the same, it's important to remember that your

actions are only half the undertaking. The other half is to make yourself available to the actions of others.

When I was a little girl, I always loved the story *Snow White and Rose Red*. In it, two little girls, home alone on a winter's evening, heard a loud knock on the door. Somewhat afraid, they nevertheless opened it to discover a gigantic bear, his thick fur frozen with icicles.

The bear asked if he might come in. Taken aback once again, the girls did, cautiously, let him come in. He lay down beside the warm fire and went to sleep. After many days, the girls became accustomed to him. They played with his fur; they rolled around with him on the floor. He stayed with them there for many a month, until spring came; and when it grew warm, he asked for his leave and departed into the woods. Not long after, as you might guess, a handsome prince appeared at the door—the bear become man—and by autumn one of the girls was married to him.

As this charming story shows, availability is openness on every level. It means that as opportunities and persons present themselves (even if they're bears), you make yourself available to what might happen. It shows that you need to be accessible in all the usual ways: hoping, looking for an appropriate man or woman; and also by responding to whatever possible unique invitations may be presented to you—entertaining a bear, for example, for his winter's hibernation.

The Paradox of Availability

Being available also requires living in the paradox of accepting things exactly as they are, while consciously enacting the behaviors that demonstrate how much you want everything to change. It consists of leading your usual life in a state of absolute trust and comfortableness—"Here I am, leading my life, doing my job, enjoying my friends, taking my dog for a walk"—while at the same time saying, "I'm not just going to lead my regular life. I'm going to step out of my pattern and do something different."

There's a very elegant balance here; you have to do everything you've always done and also do something completely different. I have a very successful friend in her fifties who says that when she turned thirty, she decided that every year from then on, she was going to do at least one thing she'd never done before—preferably something a little scary—so she wouldn't get stuck in a rut.

If you're really looking for love, it would make good sense to follow my friend's example. That's because, in order to be receptive to love, you need to be in a state of absolute comfortableness with your life as it is, while also being willing to change anything in it. It's that paradox that constitutes availability, and when you embrace it you can stand gracefully on the tightrope of your balancing act, trusting you'll make it across the wire. So do everything you've always done *and* do something completely out of character, something crazily wonderfully different: learn how to tango, take a hiking trip to Europe, ride a motorcycle, go hot air ballooning.

All this daring reminds me of a television producer who was at the apex of her career. She was very distressed by the fact that she couldn't seem to bring love into her life. When I first met her, she'd just received a major promotion, but was feeling strangely depressed. "I can go on doing what I'm doing, and I'll continue to be successful," she said, "but what about love? These 90-hour work weeks don't leave much time for romance."

She considered other, less stressful jobs, but when the wild hair of an idea to go to Samoa to make a documentary was brought to her one Wednesday afternoon, by Friday she'd made the decision to go, and by the following week she was on the plane.

Within two weeks of her arrival, she met an attorney on location, an intelligent, kind, adventurous man unlike any she'd ever met in all the high-powered days of her stellar career. They fell in love quite quickly, were married on the island, and now have returned to the States to start a family.

This is a lovely example of how both doing the same thing you've always done (being the zebra you've always been) but deciding also to do something different (taking a stroll down the desert to see what new sassy zebras might be out there under the trees) can lead to a beautiful ending. That's why it's important to be both authentically yourself in the context where you normally are, while at the same time trying something new and completely outrageous, the sort of thing that will make people say, "I can't believe *you* did that!"

It's in these out-of-character moments that you suddenly get connected with the divine spark, the daring, trusting imaginative part of yourself. In moments of such passionate departures, a world of new possibilities looms.

The reason it's so important to live this paradox is that we never do know where love is going to come from. Love is a miracle that arrives both because of the asking and in spite of the asking, *because* of the preparation and completely apart from it. You do have to cover the waterfront, cover all the bases, try all the tricks, and buy all the lottery tickets.

That's the side of the paradox that's an effort. But then, on the other side, there's a surprising effortlessness when love just seems to show up out of the blue. There's an old saying that the bluebird of happiness may be right in your own backyard, and I've heard many a wonderful tale of people who've fallen in love with the person who was right in their midst—a friend they'd known for years, a clerk in a store they frequented, the man who worked in the office next door—whom they'd never considered as a potential lover or mate.

Here's a story about never knowing when the obvious

will strike. A woman in her 40s, recently widowed, went to her high school reunion and ran into her high school sweetheart. Seeing him once again after all those years, she remembered all the delightful feelings of their adolescent love, and felt free to tell him the story of the recent loss of her husband. She then went home and completely forgot about him.

Meanwhile, he'd been in the process of leaving a marriage in which he'd been unhappy for years. Seeing her at the reunion rekindled his feelings for her. It was amazing, he thought, that here they were, all these years later, both available and mature enough to really enjoy one another. Some time after his divorce was final, he called her up for a date. She was amused and surprised. As she told her best friend a few days later, "I can't quite believe it. This guy I broke up with in high school just called me up for a date. Isn't that ridiculous?"

Since they'd parted by a sort of mutual agreement when they'd gone off to college on opposite sides of the country, they'd never quite realized that the connection underlying their high-school romance was actually very deep. The end of this story, of course, is that after taking off her blinders to the fact that a miracle could be right in her midst, this woman surrendered to the wonderful love that had been in the making for 25 years.

True availability, as you can see, is a many-splendored thing. It includes all the things that every dating and flirting handbook can tell you, as well as opening the deepest reaches of your soul to the unexpected miracle—which may already be standing right in front of you.

Activating Your Availability

As you contemplate the matter of your own availability, it would be helpful to answer the following questions:

- In general, does it feel like you're available?

- What concrete actions can you take to embody the invitation to love that your heart longs to give? Is there an opportunity waiting (like that trip to Samoa)? Is there a club to join, a party to attend?

- How can you change your house, your heart, your work, and your behavior patterns to be more internally available to love?

As you contemplate your answers to these questions, select one change and make a commitment to enact it, whether that's a change in your behavior (I'll stop smoking—it keeps me isolated; I'll invite the guy next door over for dinner), developing a new skill (I'll learn scuba diving; I'll join a gym and start working out), sprucing up your environment (I'll buy an aquarium; I'll start raising orchids; I'll paint the living room blue), or learning how to communicate (I'll reveal myself more in every conversation; I'll tell all my friends I'm looking for love).

To reinforce your decision, I suggest selecting an object to serve as a reminder. It needn't be expensive—a ring, a bracelet, a medal, a mirror, a beautiful stone from the beach—just something to wear or keep in a prominent place. The point of this object is to concretize your commitment to take one more step toward making yourself available. Each time you look at it, it will say back to you: That's right, you're open; you're available; you're really ready to fall in love.

$\mathcal{I}$ntention

. . . .
If one advances confidently in the direction
of his dreams, and endeavors to live the life
which he has imagined, he will meet with a
success unexpected in common hours.

–*Henry David Thoreau*
. . . .

*I*ntention is consciousness strongly formed and deeply held; a wanting of the heart delivered to the mind to hold—no matter what, in spite of everything, against all obstacles, controversy or attack, from without or within. Intention is staking your claim on something that hasn't yet revealed itself, and through the staking of that claim, causing it to make its face known. Intention is the way we stand at attention, bow down before what can become of ourselves and our lives. It's the way we salute the future by imagining it.

Intention means I want; I will; I mean to; it is my purposeful plan to create; I direct my heart to these feelings; I will walk this way; I will occupy this place.

We know that "The road to hell is paved with good intentions." What is meant by this, is that intentions, half-baked, result in the frustrated outcomes that hell symbolizes. Conversely, intentions clearly stated and steadfastly held deliver us to the heaven of dreams actualized. Good intentions fulfilled are joy.

Intention is an ongoing process. It's not a single pinpointed moment in time in which we casually want, desire, hope, or imagine, but the ongoing sculpted direction of our consciousness, which is reshaped again and again as we move through life.

When we intend well, what we have imagined and believed *will* come to pass. Intention isn't a flighty little undertaking, something we can halfheartedly put our minds to. It represents, rather, the honing of priorities, the taking of a stand for what we want and are willing to stake our lives on, not just for a moment, but continuously, throughout the evolving future. Intention is also the *practice* of intention, of enacting what we have in mind again and again and again until it becomes true not only internally, but also in the outside world.

Intention is the grit of our preparation for the arrival of love. It's the emotional workout through which, each time we want to lose faith or are blown out of the water by despair, we instead marshal our energies to once again take a stand around the focus that is our intention. Unlike faith, which is quietly spiritual in nature, intention is the action of our hearts and souls in consciously seeking love. It says, not just once, but with steadfast repetition, "This is what I want; this is what I need; this is what I'm not going to give up on until it shows up in my life. I'm taking up a position and I'm not budging from my spot."

Your intention in wanting love is the backbone, the force, that will allow it to finally come to you. If you don't intend to be loved, you never will be, and if you hold your intention unwaveringly, love will absolutely be yours.

3. Know Your Real Self

Everything worth having costs something, and the price of true love is self-knowledge. It is for this reason that really becoming acquainted with yourself is a price well worth paying for the love that really will address your needs.

Knowing yourself is having more than a passing acquaintance with the person you vaguely imagine yourself to be and whose preferences you casually recognize: Yes, I like football; no, I don't like red chilies. Knowing yourself is making the effort to come into a deep awareness of your emotional being, who you truly are as a person. This includes having the courage to study your emotional makeup, to discover what hurts and delights you, what you're afraid of, what makes you happy, as well as identifying some of your main relationship needs.

You can begin this process of self-knowledge with something as simple as becoming aware of whether you're an introvert or an extrovert. Are you a person who likes to spend a lot of time sitting in the warm bath water of your own quiet company, or are you someone who likes to come out and be wildly expressive in a crowd? Are you a party person or a hermit?

Apart from being an introvert or an extrovert, what kind of lifestyle do you aspire to? Do you smoke or not? Drink alcohol or not? Are you a vegetarian? A movie fanatic? A couch potato or an exercise maniac? Do you need to spend time in nature? Listening to music? In meditation? Playing with your nephew? Visiting your parents?

It's important to know these things when you're looking for a mate so you don't present yourself with a kind of false advertising. We all have opportunities to meet people in circumstances that aren't truly reflective of who we are. The woman who meets her sweetheart at the office Christmas party when he's wearing a tuxedo, but he really hasn't been out of sweatpants for more than 24 hours in the last 20 years is getting a false impression. She may think, "Ah, here at last is a man who can bring some class to my life," when the truth is, he can't wait to get home and change back into sweats. For this reason, it's worthwhile, as you're getting acquainted with someone, to reveal who you are in some of these seemingly trivial departments.

The reason all these things are so important is that they're reflections of our emotional makeup. We each have a unique emotional makeup, which is the sum of our basic nature plus the vast array of our emotional responses, reactions, and adaptations to all the persons, experiences, and things that have touched us in our lives. These emotional reactions are continually recorded in our conscious and unconscious minds. They are our particular way of responding to a chord that was sounded long ago in our lives, and that, like a melody we once heard, comes back to haunt us time and time again.

This melody is what I call your life theme. Your life

theme refers to a way in which you were treated, a tragedy that befell you, a loss you experienced, a particular attitude that was the hallmark of your rearing as a child that affected you deeply when it originally occurred, and that has been played out time and again to a greater or lesser degree in your subsequent relationships.

Your various emotional reactions are the way you express your responses to the content of your life theme. These reactions were created in childhood and now have become an instinctive part of your being. That's why, in a very real sense, your life theme dictates who you are, why you react the way you do, and why you prefer certain people and experiences and try to avoid others. It's crucial that you understand it, because, in a very real sense, it's running your life.

Understanding Your Life Theme

I've always loved the sonata form of music. In the first part, a melodic theme—a few exquisitely beautiful notes, a musical phrase—is introduced. This is followed, in part two, by variations, which are an expansion on this theme, and finally, in the third and concluding portion, the original theme is revisited and resolved.

In a sense, we're all living sonata-form lives, being born with an original theme, playing out an endlessly repeating cycle of variations on that theme, and finally, as we conclude our lives, enacting one or another kind of resolution to this theme. Understanding your life theme is crucial, not only for self-awareness, but also for any successful relationship. For it is inevitable that each of us will play out this theme throughout our lives. Indeed your very choice of a mate and your subsequent dance with him or her is a playing out of a part of that theme.

These themes are rooted in our family histories. Neglect, separation, loss, poverty, abuse, abandonment, rejection, emotional suffocation, and fear of annihilation are all prominent life themes. In any given life, one of these themes is the sounding chord of childhood, and for the rest of that life we attempt to identify, and ultimately resolve, the painful puzzle introduced by that theme. The working out of this theme is the essence of being alive in the human form and is the psychological task we are undertaking in this lifetime.

Around each of these themes, like the spokes of a wheel, are all the emotional issues that have created areas of extreme emotional sensitivity for each of us. These are the things that can make your buzzer go off at a moment's notice because they tap into the pain of your life theme; for example, someone's perpetual lateness making you feeling abandoned once again. Or, they may represent the things you want to avoid at all costs, such as feeling angry about having to report your whereabouts, because it makes you feel smothered the way you felt as a child. As a consequence of your life theme, there may be patterns of behavior you wish to develop, such as making a cozy home to make up for the alcoholic chaos of your childhood, and others you want to let go of, such as being afraid about money all the time.

Your emotional reactions may be as ordinary as finding yourself in a jealous tizzy when your sweetheart is staring at the curvaceous calves of the tall brunette at the Chamber of Commerce mixer, because you could never get your father's attention. Or they may be as strangely odd as having a hysterical fit when your sweetheart eats the last piece of meat on the platter without first offering it to you, because it reminds you of your childhood where ten children were scrambling for the last pork chop.

Whether positive or negative, these points of sensitivity may appear ridiculous or strange to other people. But they're real to you and they can't be ignored. No matter who we are, we all have these major themes and a constellation of emotional sensitivities around them; and our life's emotional journey is becoming aware of and working through them. To the degree that you're already aware of these emotional sinkholes, you can protect yourself (and your new love) from being undermined by these cloaked monsters of the unconscious, which show up when you least expect them, and to the degree that you're not, they will surface to be addressed in your relationship.

Consciously identifying your life theme and emotional sensitivities is, therefore, of the utmost importance; and disclosing them to the person with whom you're forming a new relationship can be a way of creating emotional intimacy between you. It will also make you both aware of what the areas of sensitivity in your relationship are likely to be and, as a consequence, where you might find yourselves repeatedly working on problems.

Life Themes in Action

To begin to get a sense of what your life theme might be, you might look at your most characteristic behaviors. For we often deal with our themes by compensating for them: My father rejected me so I became an overachiever; my mother gave me up for adoption so I became emotionally dependent. They can also be played out by withdrawing: My mother overwhelmed me, so I became commitment phobic, my father criticized me, so I became passive-aggressive. More serious adaptations to the difficulties of early life themes include depression, personality disorders, avoidance through addiction, codependence, and submerging emotional issues through overintellectualizing.

To see how these life themes operate, let's look at Fred and Ethel. Fred was the son of an aggressive tyrannical father and a kind, retiring mother, who was also squashed and intimidated by Fred's raging father.

Fred's life theme was rejection, and, as a consequence, uncertainty about his power as a man. He was male, but his model for maleness was unacceptable to him. He didn't want to be like his angry father, but he also didn't want to be like his mother, run over by the person who supposedly loved her. These were his areas of emotional sensitivity.

For many years Fred handled his rejection (and fear of being a man) by becoming a non-achiever, drinking to excess, and avoiding all emotional involvements where conflict with the other person might arise. After gingerly sampling a series of relationships where he didn't get squashed, Fred decided to give up drinking altogether, and attempt success at a "real job," where he finally met Ethel. Her willingness to appreciate him as the gentle man he was, rather than the aggressive beastly man he was afraid of becoming, allowed him to integrate his sensitivity with his strength. Although he is still sensitive to conflict and still defining his own appropriate male image, Fred has come a long way in resolving his life theme.

Ethel was the daughter of a hysterical, abusive, alcoholic mother who in drunken rages would threaten her young daughter's life. Her father, a traveling salesman, was rarely home and left Ethel to cope with her explosive out-of-control mother. Ethel's life theme was fear of annihilation.

Her emotional issues were all centered around feeling unprotected and therefore at risk. Her coping mechanisms were to be a perfect child (and thereby avoid setting off her mother's wrath), accommodating and pacifying others, and withdrawing to her room to read. As an adult an unkind look or word, or a highly or somewhat explosive situation with friends or at work, could put her literally in a panic state.

As she went through several relationships which replicated her mother's explosiveness, she gradually faced her fear and became stronger in the presence of the many things that could set it off. When she met Fred, his quiet nature and kindness as well as the strength he exhibited in giving up his addiction all made her feel safe and loved.

What's significant about the success of their relationship is that by the time they found each other they were both well acquainted with their life theme and the ways it had affected them. They were also able to communicate about it. Now that we've looked at Fred and Ethel, let's take a look at you for a moment:

- What is your life theme? Of the major themes—emotional or physical neglect, a family pattern of mental or physical illness, loss through death, feeling like an outcast, being emotionally invaded, poverty, physical or emotional abuse, physical or emotional abandonment, rejection of your true nature, fear of annihilation, emotional suffocation—which one most applies to you?

Although life themes are extremely powerful, intuitively, we're all trying to move beyond the pain they hold for us to the joy that is represented by love and union. The more you can be consciously aware of your theme and the sensitivities you have as a consequence, the more you will be able to resolve your emotional issues. As the painful issues around your life theme are gradually worked through, they will start to recede. You will enjoy your love relationships more and a new relationship can be about personal fulfillment rather than yet another reenactment of the painful themes of your early life.

It's true, of course, that we discover many of these deep issues only through our intimate relationships. You may not know you have an issue of jealousy, for example, until you really fall in love. Suddenly you're vulnerable, and only then may the prospect of impending loss hit you in a way it never did when you were just having a casual relationship. While some issues become visible only through the magic mirrors of actually being in a relationship, others are so gigantic they step into our relationships with us, blaring our life themes like trumpets. In either case, they live with us like our shadows, and as we expose them to the pure light of day, their hold on us diminishes.

The Beauty of Our Limitations

As we've begun to see, there is a set of coping behaviors we each develop in response to our life themes as a way to survive. Among them are: withdrawal, manipulation, panic, hysteria, inability to make a commitment, passive-aggression, and overintellectualizing. Each of these represents an attempted solution to the pain of our life theme; unfortunately, they can also be problematic in an intimate relationship. They can create a barrier to love or be the source of repetitive conflicts.

Yet ironically they also serve to draw our partners to us. The beauty of our limitations is that they represent the places where we need to grow, where we need to be healed and loved. Intuitively we seek out the person who can provide this healing; and intuitively the person who can provide this healing is also drawn to us.

Indeed, a very important part of any relationship is this healing process. It begins in frustration as limitations surface, becomes a test of the mettle of love as these difficulties are worked with, and becomes a victory of transformation when true healing occurs.

This process is always enhanced by the degree of consciousness with which it is undertaken. If you're aware of your limitations, your blow-out points and super-vulnerabilities, you can bring them to the table of your relationship for healing. If you refuse to bring them up to the light of awareness, however, you run the risk of having them be the reason your relationship can't get off first base, or comes to a grinding halt.

Nobody is without one or more of these difficult foibles of personality. They are in fact the uniqueness that make us interesting as individuals. But they cause us problems too. As we go through life, we discover again and again that these particular traits are the sand-paperish source of difficulty in all our love relationships. Whatever was irritating to one partner will be irritating to others. And, since none of us is without our own bouquet of imperfections, we might as well start right now, being realistic about them.

So have a moment of candor with yourself. To begin to get at your own limitations:

- List five or six very specific odd areas that are emotionally sensitive to you, the things that can always make you angry or afraid, that drive you crazy or push your buttons. (For example, when someone's late; when someone doesn't say thank you; when someone raises his or her voice, even in excitement; when someone makes plans to leave you for the weekend.)

- What specific behaviors do you engage in to try to find emotional comfort: nail biting, overeating or drinking, worrying about your health, depression, motor-mouthing, complaining, hysterical outbursts, tearful outbursts, shyness, cynicism, humor, silence, moodiness, exercise mania?

Whatever your irritating adaptive behaviors are, you've probably been accused of them before, and all your accusers weren't wrong. It's important to remember that whatever irritating things other people have had the courage to point out about you—your parents, siblings, colleagues, or school mates—they're most likely true. If 14 people have told you you're disorganized, they're probably right. If 49 people have told you you're never on time and it irritates the hell out of them, the person you're going to meet now will probably also have a reaction to your tardiness.

What are the things in you that make you the imperfect being who's not only a joy but also a trial to love? I'm reminded here of the Navajo Indians, who in weaving a rug, always make a conscious decision to weave in an error. It's their way of saying that only God can create perfection and everything human is tainted by a flaw.

So it is with each of us. Each of us has one or a bundle of rough edges, which are our life's work to smooth out and our partners' challenge to embrace with kindness, endure with patience, and respond to with abiding love.

As you contemplate stepping into a relationship, be realistic about who you are. Being realistic about your limitations is an act of self-love; it shows that you love yourself just as you are. It will allow you also to open your arms and your heart to the person who, just like you, still isn't quite perfect.

Circumstantial Limitations

Along with recognizing your cornucopia of emotional limitations, it's important to realize that you also have circumstantial limitations. These are certain things over which you really have no control: the fact that your landlord's kicked you out of your apartment and you don't have a bedroom in which to entertain your new beau; the fact that your company's decided to move you on a minute's notice to the other side of the country; or that your mother's had an emergency appendectomy, and it's up to you to nurse her through her recovery.

At any given moment, we may each have specific circumstances that can impinge on our availability. We may have goodwill and sweetness of spirit, but our circumstances may be such that we're not available for the banana split of love, we have only enough time for the one-scoop ice cream cone.

Circumstantial limitations are real. They're part of what you arrive with as you walk up to the doorstep of love. They're not your fault—they're beyond your control—but it's important that you acknowledge them without fudging as you present yourself. If you don't, they'll surface anyway—unpleasantly—and they could very quickly become the reason your relationship doesn't get off the ground.

To check yourself out in the circumstantial limitations department, answer the following question:

- What are your present circumstantial limitations to having a relationship? Recovering from an injury that requires physical therapy 20 hours a week; having to spend all your time rebuilding your house after a fire; being a traveling salesperson who's home only a few days each month?

We all have hell times, when all we can do is put one foot in front of the other and try to keep walking. Such impediments don't necessarily imply that you shouldn't get involved at all, merely that you be honest with yourself and your potential beloved about the truth of your conditions, and how they're likely to impinge on your possible partnership.

Facing the truth—and talking about it—can be a source of real intimacy. If your circumstances are such that it isn't really wise for you to get into a serious relationship right now, it would be kind of you to say that. And who knows? Perhaps the person you're dating would be happy with your particular circumstances. Maybe he or she has circumstances of their own, that makes yours a perfect fit. For example, I know a traveling salesman who fell in love with a woman who had just recently been divorced. The fact that he was around only intermittently allowed her to go through the grieving process in solitude. She was able to complete it in his absence, and he was spared being inappropriately involved in the resolution of her previous relationship.

What Are Your Gifts?

Along with knowing your limitations, it's important to know your positive attributes. What is your personal dowry, the riches you bring to a relationship?

Because so many of us are fragile in our self-confidence and because so few of us have been appropriately encouraged in the process of self-creation, we're often aware only of our limitations. They're spelled out to us all too graphically by thoughtless parents, nasty schoolmates, disgruntled ex-spouses. Often it's our gifts, the beauty and power that resides in our personal selves, that elude us.

We live in a culture that doesn't really allow us to honor the depth, strength, and exquisite uniqueness that we each possess. It's almost as if we can show our true colors only through some achievement that society acknowledges—climbing up some corporate ladder or other, making a certain number of thousands of dollars. As a result, most of us don't have the ability to see ourselves as the gifted people we are, or to know the intricate, ever-changing kaleidoscopic nuances of our greatest attributes as individuals.

Some of your gifts are the consequence of very deliberate preparations, such as getting a massage license, so you are able to give a wonderful back rub, while others are gifts of the soul that have been in the making for aeons—patience or gentleness of spirit, for example. What we have to offer isn't always what we know we have to offer, but if you look carefully, you'll be able to recognize your gifts. They are your essence, your personal beauty and uniqueness.

In addition, because we're all in a state of constant evolution, you're in a place now where what you have to offer may be different from what it was several relationships ago. You may say, "Well, now that I have my emotional traumas sorted out, I can be a conscious, communicating partner." Or, "Now that I've solved the riddle of my asthma, I'm ready to be a mother." Or, "Now that I have my Ph.D., I'm ready to become the bread winner."

As you prepare yourself for the love of your life to come in, think about what you have to offer. What are your riches, the basket of treasures you have to share? Consider the following:

- What is it about you that makes you worth loving and a joy to love? Do you have a quick wit, a beautiful body, a kindly heart, the ability to bring out the best in others? Do you have a gift for business? Are you a healer? Do you have courage? Directness of speech? A beautiful voice? A gift with music?

- What is your favorite thing about yourself?

- What are you consistently praised for that you know is special about you?

- What is the state of being you have brought yourself to—for example, equanimity, willingness to communicate, openheartedness—that is now your treasure to share in a way that you never have before?

As you look over your answers to all these questions, do you see what a treasure you are and what you have to offer? It's time to lay claim to the beauty of yourself and not be embarrassed by the grand riches you possess. Knowing what is strong and beautiful in you, whether you were born with it or developed it though suffering or other effort, is attracting to you at this very moment the person who is your perfect counterpart.

How Do You Want To Be Loved?

Along with facing our limitations and our gifts, it's also important to know how, exactly, we'd like to be loved. We all have secret scenarios of what circumstances, words, ways, ambiences, and environments add up to love for us. These change from time to time: Sometimes your need for security may be greatest, at other times it may be your need for deep emotional contact; but overall there are certain experiences and behaviors that, if you receive them, will generate in you the feeling of truly being loved.

If you don't know by now at least some of what constitutes this for you, it will be difficult to recognize love when it comes along. So think about what your love preferences are, and write down your answers to the following:

- What is it that really makes you feel loved? Is it the things you hear, the way you're touched, the looks you receive?

- What are the exact words you'd like to hear? The touches you want to feel? The looks you'd like to be looked at with?

- How would you like the person who loves you to honor the gifts you bring to a relationship? By telling you? By writing you cards? By providing for you? Making love to you? Smiling with joy every time he encounters some beautiful aspect of you? Thanking God for you? Telling all her friends about you? Advertising your great love on e-mail? Whispering to you at night about how wonderful you are?

- Where would you like to live out your love:
  Your apartment? His apartment? A house you share? A
  boat? A hut in the tropics? Many airplanes and hotels? A
  small town close to your parents? As far away from your
  parents as you can possibly get? In the city? In the country? Where it snows? Where it's warm?

Once you've made your list, put it in an envelope, tuck it
away somewhere and wait to see what happens. The mere
fact that you've written these things down will make your
intention beam stronger.

A Symphony of Emotional Interchange

All these facets of self-awareness—knowing your life theme,
being honest about your limitations, celebrating your vir-
tues, and being aware of how you want to be loved—are
what will make you not only a viable but a radiant candidate for a loving relationship. For, when it comes to falling
in love, nothing is more important than who we are and
what we know about ourselves emotionally.

That's because intimate relationships are emotional interactions. They inspire our feelings; they heal our emotional wounds; they are a symphony of emotional interchange
where we play out our fear, delight, disappointment, cha-
grin, excitement, passion, outrage, hope, and sorrow on a
daily basis.

Intention

Emotions are the grist for every relationship mill. They show us who we are; they lead us to who we are becoming. To the degree that you are consciously acquainted with your emotional self, have peace with it, and can present it with integrity, to that degree you are prepared for the joy, harmony, and company of an intimate relationship.

4. *Discover* Why Love Has Eluded You

It may seem like a complete mystery that you don't have love in your life right now. But it's not. That's because underlying the presence or absence of a relationship in your life are some unconscious motivators that are helping create the very situation you find yourself in.

You may be consciously saying to yourself, "I want to fall in love; why doesn't somebody come along and sweep me off my feet?" but the truth is, other things, of which you may not be consciously aware, are also operating. When we bring these forces into conscious awareness, we can see how we have been inhibiting ourselves from finding love. By bringing these issues to light, we become able to meet the person we will love to love.

Indeed, the truth about why you're not in a relationship right now consists of a number of factors both within and outside of your control. Among the ones you can affect are the psychological and circumstantial reasons hidden in the veiled chambers of your clever unconscious. The reasons you may have for not being in the kind of relationship you say you want include relationship ambivalence, circumstantial conflicts, an incomplete recovery from a previous relationship, and the fear of facing your deepest fears. First, let's look at ambivalence.

Just Because You Asked for It Doesn't Mean You Want It

There isn't a person on the face of the earth who doesn't have *some* ambivalence about being in a relationship. That's because we want to be in love and yet we're also in the process of trying to create ourselves as individuals. Intuitively, we know that our own uniqueness is the most precious gift we've received. We've each been given the tribute of being a distinct, unrepeatable human being in our own unique garb of body, face, soul, and emotions. Thus, as we go through the process of life, we are very focused on who we are as individuals—trying to figure ourselves out, to become exactly who we were meant to be, to enjoy ourselves to the fullest, to develop ourselves to the maximum.

At the same time, we also have a deep longing for connection, for the dissolution of our boundaries, for melting belonging. We don't want to be alone with our marvelous selves; we want to be connected to another human being, to swim into a bondedness that is juicy, exquisite, and sweet. And so, as we pass through our lives, we're like slightly schizophrenic personalities who on the one hand want to be absolutely sure we get to be who we are, while at the same time we want to throw caution and our uniqueness to the wind, and melt into a gooey pool of belonging with somebody else.

Because of this ongoing dichotomy, we all experience ambivalence. Intuitively we recognize that a relationship isn't simply an experience of total self-indulgence where we get everything we want on a silver platter and don't have to go through any compromises or heartaches.

We're not stupid. We all know that any relationship will involve compromise, the taking into account of another human being in all his or her uniqueness, complexity, and demandingness, and with all of his or her psychological baggage, irritating habits, and idiosyncracies. Even the man or woman of our dreams is going to have noisome little quirks we're going to have to deal with. Because we know this, we're ambivalent. We'd like to fall in love, but we know it's not going to be a piece of cake, a walk in the park, or that ever-elusive bowl of cherries.

However, the degree to which this ambivalence has been developed varies greatly from one person to another. But in most cases, it centers around either a fear of abandonment or a fear of being overwhelmed.

If you were abandoned, for example, you may feel very strongly about wanting the closeness and companionship that a relationship promises. At the same time, you may also want never to risk possible abandonment again; thus your ambivalence may be really strong. You may find yourself dancing into a relationship with one foot and sashaying out of it with the other. It's as if a little voice in your unconscious keeps saying, "I know what it's like to loved and left, and I'm never going to put myself in that kind of jeopardy again. I'd like to be loved, but this is too scary."

Similarly, if you grew up feeling overwhelmed in a family of 12 children, you may say on the one hand, "I've had enough of togetherness. Give me some privacy and solitude." At the same time, perhaps you treasure the closeness you experienced in those early years and are therefore deeply drawn to having an intimate relationship. Herein lie the makings of a profound ambivalence.

What I'm saying here is that the particular configuration of one's childhood issues doesn't precisely predict the kind of ambivalence you will have or the degree to which it will operate. That's because your ambivalence depends upon the particular emotional coping strategies you developed. The important thing to remember is that there is a unique but deeply embedded dose of relationship ambivalence in all of us. It's important to be aware of it, because it's operating all the time, and as you stand mindlessly waiting for someone to love to show up, it will definitely be playing its part.

I say mind*lessly* waiting because when you wait mind*fully* for love to come in, you hold the awareness of these conflicts in the forefront of your consciousness. Then, if at precisely the moment you meet the person who really is right to fall in love with and you feel like running like hell, you can say to yourself, "Ah, there's my ambivalence. Hello there, I remember you. You're what always stands in my way when I have a chance to fall in love; you raise all my objections and fears. But you know what, this time I'm going to step right over you and fall in love anyway, because this person's worth taking the risk for."

One more thing about ambivalence—it's okay to feel it, although that's not what the common wisdom says. If you want to fall in love, the P.R. goes, you've got to want to do it one hundred percent. Unfortunately, it's precisely because we don't acknowledge our ambivalence that we often allow it to sabotage our relationships or to prevent us from getting into them in the first place.

If you wonder about the true power of ambivalence to direct your relationship path, here's a story that really brings it home. Claire was a client who seemed perennially on a quest for love. A successful young woman in her thirties, she had been married briefly in her twenties to a man whose work required him to be out of the country for more than half of each year. Her own work, being a sales rep for a record company, took her out of town for weeks at a time. For the entire duration of their two-and-a-half-year marriage she and her husband barely spent more than three consecutive weeks together. When they divorced, Claire attributed the failure of the marriage to the fact that the two of them never spent any time together.

She stated that her goal in therapy was to meet a man and get married. She also said that for the past year she had conducted "a major campaign to find a man," but that it had been unsuccessful. She had written and answered numerous personals ads, joined a number of clubs for singles, and taken singles vacations. But all these efforts had only resulted in an endless string of unsatisfying romances varying in length from a week to several months.

It wasn't until she was able to bring up to consciousness the fact that she had been sexually abused by her brother that she was able to make the connection that she was unconsciously sabotaging each relationship opportunity that came to her. It just wasn't safe for her to be in an ongoing intimate circumstance with a man. As she worked through the painful feelings around her abuse, she was gradually able to step through her fears and risk more in each relationship, until, I'm delighted to report, two years ago she was happily married.

This story isn't to say that if you're alone you've been sexually abused, but to encourage you to begin to contemplate the underlying reasons you may have for being alone. There are always some.

Take the Ambivalence Test

So let's take a look for a moment at your own relationship ambivalence. If you're alone now, no matter what your P.R. may be about wanting a relationship, step aside from what you *think* you feel and allow yourself to see what your relationship ambivalence might be. To see if you have issues with abandonment or feeling overwhelmed, ask yourself the following questions:

- Was I abandoned in childhood through adoption, or a prolonged separation from or death of a parent? Was there some other, less obvious abandonment I may not be aware of—an older sibling leaving, an alcoholic or workaholic parent, too many brothers or sisters so I never got enough attention—that's affecting my ability to really choose a relationship?

- Was one or both of my parents so overly involved with me, so demanding or emotionally invasive that I have a fear of being overwhelmed that is undermining my willingness to be intimate?

- Were you shamed, or sexually or physically abused in childhood, and if so, how afraid are you of being violated or abused again?

Be honest with yourself as you explore these questions and see if you can gain a clue as to the nature of the resistance you might be creating. Then, to get a realistic sense of how much ambivalence you might be experiencing, ask yourself the following:

- At this point, on a scale of one to a hundred, what percentage of me really wants to be in a relationship and what percentage of me wants to follow my own star home?

- How much of my freedom am I willing to give up? One, two days a week? Happy to share all my time and space?

- How much of my resources am I willing to throw into

the pot of a new relationship—My house? My car? My bank account? My circle of friends?

A man in his 30s responded to these questions by saying, "I'm only now realizing how completely controlled and overrun I was by my mother. I've experienced similar feelings in several relationships, and I see that I'm not willing to share my time or resources with someone else. Right now my priority is myself and my emotional work, to learn how to set the boundaries I'll need to be able to be happy in love."

As you can see from this person's response, answering these questions will give you a realistic profile of how your ambivalence is operating, which will prevent it from sabotaging your desire to be in a relationship. Once you see what it is and how strong it might be, don't expect it to vanish, but realize that you don't have to let it run your life when you're trying to fall in love.

Do You Really Need to Be Alone Right Now?

Relationship ambivalence isn't the only reason why you might not be in a relationship. At certain times in your life, you may need or want to be alone. There are plenty of good reasons why you might not have enough amps available for the undertaking of an intimate relationship. As one divorced father in his 40s said to me recently, "I just don't have the energy to have a relationship right now, because I'm putting all my attention on my daughter. She's about to go away to college, and since I've neglected her in the past, I really want to be able to focus on her."

Intuitively we all know that a relationship is work—and I don't mean here the work that couples often speak of when they talk about "working on" a relationship when it's gone awry and real effort is required to bring it back on track. I'm speaking here simply of the energy one expends in the undertaking of experiencing another human being emotionally, intellectually, sexually, and spiritually.

For all a relationship can bring to us, it also involves an expenditure of energy. In our best selves, we want to be able to be generous with that energy. We want to have the time and the availability of spirit that allows us to bring ourselves wholeheartedly to the work and play of being with another person. A degree of realism about this energetic investment can at times make us pause and look at what our lives consist of at any given moment. In some instances, this brings us to the place of saying, "My plate is full. I really don't have energy for the concocting of a relationship."

Some people, particularly after a difficult relationship experience, may say, point blank, "Right now, I just don't want to be in a relationship, I want to be alone." But we all may feel like a relationship isn't appropriate at one time or another. Just make sure you're aware of what the truth is for you.

Above all, remember it's okay to choose to be alone for a while, even if ultimately you do want the comfort of marriage and a family. I'm thinking here of a successful young friend who, after years of being frustrated with his job in a hospital physical therapy department, decided to create a gym of his own. In order to do so, he found himself doing one full-time job to fund the creation of the gym and spending an equivalent amount of hours actually training people in it. Many times, as he was taking them through their exercise routines, people would say to him, "Your business is going so great, Kerry, when are you going to fall in love?" And he'd always say back, "Right now all my energy's taken up with this business. I hardly have time to sleep, and I certainly don't have any energy for a relationship." (A postscript: After Kerry's business had been established for a couple years, he did meet a wonderful woman—and they are now delightedly married.)

Similarly, I once knew a young, divorced mother of two boys who suffered severe injuries in a head-on car accident. Many of her friends kept encouraging her to date, hoping she would fall in love and find a partner to help her with the burden of her sons. But she would say again and again, "You just don't understand. The boys *are* my relationship now. This is all I can handle. I'm not in the mood for romance, I'd feel too conflicted about my sons."

These stories point out that there are times in our lives when circumstances truly do make the choices for us. If you're in a situation like that, don't be afraid to acknowledge it. Many times our desire for love causes us to be unrealistic and say, "I can work the two jobs and have a lover," and actually imagine that we're going to have enough energy to make this person feel nurtured and cherished.

When we live in that kind of denial, we create relationships that are disappointing, if not ultimately destructive, to ourselves and those with whom we engage in them. Nobody likes to be exhausted or shortchanged in love. So it's important to be absolutely, unflinchingly truthful with yourself about whether or not your circumstances could realistically support your being in a relationship right now.

If you find yourself on the one hand saying, "Why isn't anybody showing up for me to fall in love with?" but on the other hand, you find that you've set up a life where you actually enjoy being alone, then obviously the love you think you desire isn't going to stumble across your path. The truth is that for one reason or another—needing recovery time, wanting time for personal growth, being swamped by a particular career undertaking—you've actually created the aloneness you need right now.

Once in a while, great loves and lovers can break through these magnitudinous resistances, but most of the time they can't. Usually, if you're either actively or unconsciously resisting the incoming of love, anyone who might be in the market for a relationship with you will feel this and will, out of self-preservation, remove him or herself from the arena. The truth is that, if on any level, conscious or unconscious, you've decided you don't want to have a relationship right now, you will be broadcasting that information, and all of your possible partners will hear it in one form or another.

- What are your circumstances of the moment?

- Is your energy bank account so overdrawn that you don't have any physical or emotional energy to expend on a relationship?

Here's what one of my clients wrote as the answer to this question: "If I'm really honest with myself, I see that I don't have time for a relationship right now. I've committed all my time to my career and I'm not willing to borrow any time from my work to invest in an emotional exchange with another person. I don't want to say that I'm a workaholic, because that's a nasty thing to be, but the truth is, I've spent years developing this career, and it's what's most fulfilling to me right now. The only relationship I could handle at the moment is a very part-time relationship."

Have You Gotten Over Your Previous Relationship?

Maybe what's holding you back from finding the love of your life is not a lack of time or energy, but the fact that you're still emotionally or sexually tied to a past relationship. If this is true, it's time to clear the decks. There isn't room for new love to come into your life when that heart-shaped compartment is occupied even to a shadowy degree by someone else. Whether you have nostalgia for the good things that were or a sexual involvement you're still enacting to some degree, these threads of connection truly prevent you from being available.

Many of us are afraid of moving into the void, which is the only condition in which love can really come to us. We want to hold on to the past. As one of my friends said, "I'm so scared, I just want to keep my old worn-out slippers, even though I know if I could just throw them away I could get a pair of new dancing shoes."

Unfortunately, like my friend, many of us are so scared of the void that we'd rather cling to a half-baked, half-a-loaf lover than really let go and create the space for someone new. However, for love to come into your life, there has to be room, and for a really great love to come into your life, there has to be a great opening.

So, if this is true for you, it's time to clear the decks—get rid of your phantom lover, the married man who sees you once every three weeks, the woman you had a fling with last summer on your two-week trip to Spain. Stop mooning over those photos from your last Hawaiian vacation—the one where you fought like cats and dogs every night. Forget the girl or guy who's maybe, any day now, going to break up with somebody else.

There are lots of reasons we continue to cling to old or phantom lovers. It's scary to be out there alone, and many of us are afraid that the last half-baked lover we had might be the last lover we'll ever get. It's this attitude, though—that things don't or won't improve—that keeps us stuck and alone.

I have known literally hundreds of people who've ended relationships that 10, 50, or 80 percent of themselves really wanted to hang on to. Years later, *not a one of them* regrets ending it, and each person who's fallen in love since then is happier now than they were in their previous relationship.

Of course, in the process a lot of fears come up. Will there be another person to love me? Will I have to go through a new kind of ordeal? I'm not getting any younger— how many times can I go through this? Are you sure the bird in the bush is better than this worn-out bird I've got right here in my hands?

Nobody can absolutely guarantee that you, too, will have the perfect outcome. But your chances are zero if you don't clear the space. So, whatever your worn out slippers look like burn them up in the fireplace and look forward to the arrival of your new dancing shoes.

Is Something Still Standing in Your Way?

If you're having trouble clearing the space, it may also be that a previous relationship was so devastating that you've put up bars to falling in love again. It doesn't even have to be your last relationship that's the problem. I've found that many people are still suffering from a high school or college romance, a passionate summer interlude, or a long-ago first marriage that's still standing in their way despite a number of subsequent relationships. If you got burned and haven't faced the truth about your pain and loss, then you'll unconsciously continue to create barriers to falling in love.

Discovering how your unresolved pain is holding you back is very important in being able to create a new relationship. Until you heal from the relationship where your heart got smashed and thrashed, you will not be able to love. Once again, this involves making the unconscious conscious. The process includes facing what was so painful about that relationship and expressing your anger and grief about it.

If you have a hunch that this is what's holding you back and you want to understand, in depth, the dynamics of your ended relationship and conduct a comprehensive self-healing process, I recommend my book, *Coming Apart, Why Relationships End and How to Live Through the Ending of*

Yours. If that doesn't bring you resolution, get help from a therapist.

I've found, however, that the following questions are a good beginning. They help clear the emotional decks, so that you will be able to love wholeheartedly again:

- What is the unbearably painful thing about this particular relationship, the thing you can't seem to get over? Write a letter to the person and express this; tell all.

- Now, write the letter of response you *wish* you could have received from him or her. Notice, as you complete it, how much of your pain dissolves.

- What is the beautiful, special, irreplaceable thing you miss so much about this past relationship—the thing that still keeps you attached in your heart—the great sex, the birth of your child, backpacking, the sound of her voice, that magic psychic connection? Write all about it.

- Now, as if you were your partner, write a letter back to yourself, saying how much you also miss this connection and how much you, too, have suffered by losing it. Let yourself cry. Then notice how much more of your pain dissolves.

The truth is, we all have a choice if we've been heartbroken in the past. We can let heartbreak become the architecture of the rest of our lives (and choose a life of solitude and isolation), or we can choose to move through the old grief, heal from it, reawaken our intention, and consciously prepare ourselves to love again. If this is what's standing in your way, I hope you will have the courage to complete your healing and risk opening your heart again.

That's because you can't have true love without an open heart, and you can't have an open heart and be bitter at the same time. If you keep saying, "I can't fall in love because my last boyfriend walked out on me," or "because I found my ex-wife in bed with another man," you won't be able to fall in love. As long as these things are still highly emotionally charged for you, your heart can't be fully open.

It's true, of course, that a wonderful miracle of love can be precisely the vehicle for opening your heart. But even a great love is only a can opener, not a crowbar. If you're really determined to keep your heart closed, even an atom bomb can't blow it open.

However, an open heart is often scarred. Sometimes we think that if our hearts are scarred, they can't possibly be open, that if we've suffered the wounds of heartbreak, betrayal, loss, or grief, these are permanent disfigurements of the heart. While these tragedies do certainly leave their marks, they often make our hearts stronger: stronger in openness, stronger to be aware of what love truly is, stronger to let love in—but only if we've resolved them.

Facing Our Deepest Fears

Love may also be eluding you because you haven't faced your fear of failing. We've all had relationship failures and they scare us; we're afraid of blowing it again. We've all had experiences that make us feel like we don't have the talent, capacity, or just plain luck that will allow us to have an intimate relationship.

At times this fear of failing may have you feeling you're jinxed in love and all that you can do is fail. But what we call "failure" in love is actually growth, because even our so-called "failures" expand us. For, as you experience both the hurts and gifts that punctuate the ever-changing vicissitudes of your life of intimate relationships, you become more and more able to embrace others and yourself. Indeed, your past relationships have honed you as a lover, so don't let past relationship "failures" stand in your way.

Finally, for each of us, underlying our ambivalence and our fear of failure is our one greatest fear, which is that to love greatly is also to live in the face of possible loss. Although we don't ordinarily go around thinking about it, there's a great clamp inside us that says "I can't let myself go here, because if I do, then I'd be putting myself in the neighborhood of a bigger loss than I've ever experienced before."

I remember once speaking to a woman who'd found the man she recognized as her soul mate. She was completely blown away, she said. She'd never really believed there would be such a person. She spoke of going for a lovely walk with this man, down by the harbor one evening, and of having an absolutely idyllic time.

"The next morning the weirdest thing happened," she said. "I woke up and I was angry. It was the most shocking feeling. I thought, How can this be—I've found the man of my dreams, and the feeling I'm having is *anger.* I don't get it. Suddenly, I realized that because I was experiencing love of this incredible magnitude, I was also facing my terror of possibly losing him. It was amazing. I'd never had to think about it before. I'd never felt that strongly about anyone; so I'd never had to encounter my vulnerability; and when I did it made me angry."

In a way we're all like this woman. We may feel angry or we may feel scared, because with each love we risk loss. To love in the face of this great fear means that we open our hearts so large that even the potential loss of the person we love isn't big enough to prevent us from diving in. Nowhere does the age-old saying that it is better to have loved and lost become more beautifully true than when we step through our greatest fear and risk the bliss of real love. To be aware of this fear is to become increasingly more able to jump over it when love knocks at your door.

Honesty Is the Best Policy

As this chapter indicates, we all have a variety of unconscious scenarios that are operating as we stand, sometimes desperate and longing, at the portal to love. We're all saying we want love, but we need to recognize that other voices in other rooms are also being heard, and that they may be speaking a very different message than the obvious voice we think is directing us.

As you explore why love has eluded you, it's most important to be ruthlessly honest. We're all active participants in the reality we're living in, and while we may not always be aware of just how we're pushing the buttons and pulling the levers, the truth is that we are indeed helping to design our own lives. More than most of us are aware, we are the architects of our lives. The more we recognize this, the more we'll be able to get what we say we long for in our hearts.

. . . .

5. Develop Your Capacity for Love

Nothing can bring love to you faster than developing your own capacity to love. The truth is that love is all around us all the time; we're swimming in a great sea of love, breathing in the breath of love with every inhalation. We are all touching each other with love. Love is embodied in every person we meet, each dog who licks our hands, every goldfish that swims in our fish ponds, every bird that alights in our trees. Even a rock is love—passion and connection—to the rock climber scaling the mountain.

Stepping into the awareness that every person, moment, and experience is an opportunity to connect with the love that binds us all together is a grand and wonderful welcome to the particular form of romantic love you seek. Nobody wants to show up where they're not invited or to love when they're not feeling loved. That's why, when you're asking for that special someone to arrive, the person who will want to show up will feel much more welcome if he or she is stepping into an atmosphere of love. (Indeed, they won't be able to resist!)

That's because when you act lovingly, when you are gracious, appreciative, praising, generous, attentive, kind, a celebrator of both people and the marvels of life, you are irresistible. You become such a beam of joy and radiance that not only will people be drawn to you, you will be deluged with offers of love. For, just as water seeks its own level, love seeks its own depth.

Conversely, if you're an elitist about love, if you hold the position that nothing except the knight on the white horse or the woman who will make mad passionate love with you all night for the next thirty years can jiggle the needle on your Richter scale of love, then you're closing off the very channel in yourself through which you can attract love to you.

You can enhance your chances most effectively if, in your longing for love, you refuse to be grumpy, grouchy, or bitter, or to take on the sour demeanor that says, "Everyone else is in a relationship, why not me?" The minute you take this position, beautiful little experiences of love that are trying to gather around you will wither in your midst.

But when you allow your own loving energy to gradually expand outward to others, you'll create more opportunities for someone to be attracted to you. You'll also begin to get the gist of what this thing called love is really all about. As you start having more experiences of love, you'll begin to discover how your body feels when you're in the midst of a loving connection, how your mental outlook changes—your depression lifts, joy expands, anxiousness contracts when you're in the presence of love. And when you become an astute, kindhearted observer of your experience, you will see that hundreds of these delicate moments change you dramatically: A word of recognition gives you a beautiful sense of calm, a sweet blessing gives you a sense of well-being, a fabulous compliment lifts your spirit, a comforting hand quells the butterflies in your stomach.

Practice Makes Perfect

What I'm really saying here is that love is a process. It's not just a meteorite that falls out of the sky and plops itself in the middle of your front yard, digging in its stellar heels and saying, "I'm going to light up your life." It's the ongoing experience of practicing the spiritual and emotional traditions of an intimate relationship.

Love is an *action*. It's not something for which we're just passive receptors; we must also be the deliverers of love.

This can seem unfamiliar. It's much easier to focus on the love we want to get, rather than on the love we can start giving. But don't be like the young woman I know who died at age 43, bitter, angry, still waiting for love. "Why didn't anybody love me?" she kept asking. "Why didn't my husband love me? Why didn't my daughter love me better? Why hasn't anybody come along to love me now?" she kept saying as friends and strangers sat at her bedside, holding her hand, talking and praying, bringing her books and bouquets of flowers. On her deathbed, she was still soaked with bitterness, unavailable to the love all around her and, above all, to her own undelivered love.

So, if you find yourself in despair about love, wondering why it hasn't knocked down your door, or, God forbid, find yourself sinking into bitterness, get out of your house and go knock down someone else's door. Give your love, and instantly the love you need will start coming toward you; in fact, it will have already arrived.

You can be both a student and a teacher of love in every moment of your life. Say "hello" to strangers and smile at them; risk offering a compliment. Remember your friends with kindness and continually celebrate them. Say the things that are so obvious most people would keep them to themselves, things like, "You're so beautiful"; "It's wonderful to see you again"; "Your friendship means the world to me"; "I love the sound of your voice"; "Thank you for being the loving presence you are."

You will know you are truly living your life in the breathing, pulsating web of love when you can celebrate its every instance. So whatever small, beautiful moments are given to you—and they are given to you constantly, gratis, for absolutely no reason—whatever the thousand little miracles that sustain you through every moment of your life, take note of them; let them have an impact on you. Acknowledge all the little miracles so they become clear and vivid in your consciousness. They will prepare you for the big ones. For receiving little love is the trampoline from which you can bounce up high and reach for the big love that will truly fulfill you completely.

Risk Vulnerability

One way to start practicing love is to look at others from an attitude of curiosity rather than judgment: Who are you? What's going on with you? I wonder what tragedies shaped your life? This is quite different from saying: Why aren't you paying attention to me? When are you going to love me? or Why are you wearing that weird plaid shirt with those baggy striped pants?

When we step out of criticism and judgment and simply hold the place of openhearted observation, we're practicing love at its most elementary and gracious. This willingness to be open—as opposed to drawing conclusions, making analyses, or trying to get the definitive answer—is what prepares us for the open state in which a love of truly mind-boggling proportions can come in.

So, try to be emotionally accessible both as a giver and a receiver. Don't be afraid to ask for what you need or to respond to another's request. For example, the woman sitting next to me in the airplane last week said the minute I got situated, "I have a very bad shoulder. Would you mind getting up and trying to get me a bag of ice from the stewardess?"

She trusted me to be in a loving moment with her. She trusted my willingness to serve her as a compassionate friend. Conversely, I remember being very appreciative of the gentleman who sat beside me one night in a New York theater. I smiled at him before the lights went down, and a few minutes later he graciously said to me, "May I help you with something?" When I said, "Yes, certainly," he said, "You look lovely, but there's a big smudge of lipstick across your front teeth. I thought you might like to remove it." He was taking the risk of giving—and I of receiving—his help and this was a moment of generous connection.

Getting a bag of ice or helping someone remove a lipstick smudge aren't the greatest love gestures of a lifetime. But whenever you take a risk—a tiny one or a mountain-sized one, of either giving or receiving, whether from a stranger or someone you already know—you're opening the vast cathedral of love in yourself to which you can return to worship for a lifetime.

You're also practicing the skills you'll need when you want to move into an intimate relationship in which you will often be required to be vulnerable. When we take a small emotional risk, the risks we can subsequently take are deeper. We can say, not only "Can you get me a bag of ice for my shoulder?" but "Can you listen to my story? Can I tell you my fears, and will you comfort me?"

Along with a willingness to take emotional risks, you must also be willing to be affected by those you meet, because love is always a simultaneous process of both giving and receiving, affecting and being affected. We put love out and we take it in, and it is this completed circuit that allows us to feel love in its totality.

Part of feeling this completeness is allowing yourself to be moved by those you meet, to be affected by the human condition of others: When you see someone suffering, to be moved to compassion; when you experience someone being wonderfully generous, to be openly grateful. As you move back and forth through the counterpoint of these exchanges, you will begin to see the great accumulation of ordinary miracles that will allow you to truly believe in the constant presence of love. In other words, each fine, exquisitely rare or touchingly painful experience you encounter is an opportunity to develop your own capacity for love, either as a receiver of its benefits or as a giver of its gifts.

So, as you go through the daily routine of your life, instruct yourself to be open and to respond: to praise, celebrate, and care for, to empathize and nurture. At each moment in your life, at every juncture and in each encounter, there's an opportunity to exercise your love muscles so they'll become Olympic-gold-medal-winning quality.

Any way, place, person, creature, or experience to which you're delivering your love is enhancing your capacity to love. If your houseplants are flourishing, if your dogs and cats are happy, if your friends cherish you, you already know how to love. See how much you can expand your capacity while you're waiting for the person of your dreams to come into your life.

Show Your True Colors

When you do come across a potentially appropriate person, revealing yourself, showing your true colors, is another important way of making yourself available to love. By doing so, the person you're meeting will have a chance to discover the real you. And when you show yourself, the other person will feel more willing to reveal him or herself. This way, you get to a level of intimacy much more quickly.

To practice showing your true colors, why don't you try, from now on, in every encounter you have with a possible sweetheart, to reveal three things about yourself. These need not be gigantic revelations—a childhood trauma or your secret sexual fantasy—but simple things such as what your favorite flower is, the name of the perfume you're wearing, or the fact that you had such a lousy birthday last year that you're a little anxious about your birthday next week.

Three's a charm, so be sure to try *three* revelations: the fact that you didn't sleep well last night, that you're worried about your father's health, that you like to get up with the sun every morning. Everything you reveal becomes the basis for the decision making that another person, consciously or unconsciously, is using to evaluate you. By the same token, disclosures on the other person's part will help you to know whether to pursue the relationship further or to move on to someone else in your romantic exploration.

Whatever these little disclosures are, they serve to reveal

you as a vulnerable human being. Disclosure is the breath of the self. It is your essence being breathed out into the world where those who are in your atmosphere can gradually begin to perceive who you are. It's also an opportunity for you—in the presence of someone else—to discover your own being in ways that perhaps you hadn't understood before.

When we withhold such revelations, we present ourselves as fully finished, finely polished porcelain people who don't have cracks and flaws and who don't need to be loved (especially in the areas where we *are* cracked and flawed). Conversely, the more you disclose about yourself, the more you become visible to yourself and the person you're exploring to love.

These kernels of self-revelation are the foundation of any relationship. What we reveal about ourselves in the moment-by-moment and day-to-day of our lives—our hurts and pleasures, our aspirations and longings, even our flaws and cheap thrills—all these are the food of love. They are what keep us together through doubt, over time, and during the many seasons of change that any relationship undergoes.

Be sure it's your real self you're showing. Because it's your *real* self that needs to be loved—the one who's hurt and insecure, the one who isn't sure she's pretty enough, the one who's afraid he doesn't have a good enough job to invite a woman out to dinner. Whatever your insecurity is, it's part of your makeup, part of your beauty as a person. So don't hide your true self under a bushel.

In this regard, it's important to remember that falling in love isn't a contest to see who you can fool, but an opportunity to finally bring your real self out of the closet, to step into the presence of someone whose joy it will be to love, honor, and cherish your true, uncamouflaged self. So take that risk from the start; don't play all the little ridiculous games that you'll have to make up for later by reluctantly, embarrassingly showing your true self. Nothing is more precious, more lovable, more exciting, or more thrilling to meet than a genuine, authentic human being. So be yourself at every step of your courtship.

I'm reminded here of the story of a young woman who said she'd been looking for love for years and finally met a man who captured her interest. She invited him out to a lunch with the hope that they'd have a wonderful time. She knew he liked carnations, and so she situated herself in the restaurant where they had agreed to meet behind a huge bouquet of red carnations, which she hoped would grab his attention. From her vantage point, she could look out and see each person who entered. Finally the man came in. He looked across the restaurant, but not being able to see her (lost as she was behind her wall of red carnations), and presuming, perhaps, that she hadn't yet arrived, he went out and waited on the street. Finally, he came back in, looked futilely around the restaurant once again, and then sadly walked out the front door.

At this point, instead of making herself known, the woman decided to get irritated. "I'm not sure I like him anyway," she said to herself. "He can't even figure out that I'm hiding behind these carnations. He must be stupid." A few minutes later, she got up, left in a huff, and missed all opportunities of ever getting acquainted with this man.

To this day, she—and we—still don't know who he was. Was he a color-blind knight on a white horse? Or just an ordinary, sweet guy who couldn't figure out the elaborate test she'd prepared for him? We'll never know and neither will she. Unfortunately, when you create a test at the very beginning, you're not establishing an environment for love, you're setting up an environment of challenge and hostility.

If you're trying to find a love bird by putting vinegar on its tail, don't expect to get loved. Love likes sweetness; so if you want love to come to you, be sweet and dear and open and charming. And if you have such an interesting idea as hiding behind a bouquet of carnations, but your clever ploy misses the point, be willing to come down off your high horse and share your flowers with the person you brought them for in the first place.

Remember, if you really want to find the person of your dreams, you need to put away all those tried and untruthful manipulative maneuvers. What you get when you use such tactics is somebody who's fallen for your tactics, not a person who's here to know and love you as you really are.

Learn to Listen and Inquire

As you step into the arena where you want to enhance the chances of love's nipping at your heels, it wouldn't hurt to adopt a couple of other behaviors—listening and inquiring—which will also help love come to you. We don't often think of listening and inquiring as important capacities for love, but they are.

Listening is a risk, because when you truly listen you make yourself available to discover not only what pleases and would probably delight you, but also what might distress you about another person. Listening is an act of love that says, "I'm here to receive whatever it is you have to put out—a fact, a revelation, an attitude, or a dream—even if it makes me uncomfortable. I'm going to stand here and risk being open to you. I'm willing to be informed, charmed, scared, delighted, or changed. I'm willing to have you reveal yourself, no matter who you turn out to be."

Inquiring is listening to the ninth power. It moves listening from a place of passivity to a place of action, because when we inquire about another person, we not only exercise our lively, loving curiosity, we also take a big risk, the risk of being disappointed. We're actually saying, "I'm going to ask you about things that might be a deal-breaker for me." For example, "Why *did* you split up with your ex-husband?" or "What are your views on rearing those two little children whose lives I might be stepping into?" or "How do you feel about the fact that I'm $5000 in debt?"

When we inquire, we're taking our blinders off and saying, "I'm willing to get to know you—not just as my fantasy, but as who you actually are. I'm durable enough to discover you and to make your real acquaintance." True love is based on *real* knowing. When we courageously inquire, we demonstrate that we're willing to know the whole person, warts and all; we also indicate that we're able to move toward the things that might be difficult in a possible future relationship as opposed to avoiding them. We offer our emotional availability; in this way, inquiring is loving of the highest order.

If you learn the fine, grand, and sensitive art of loving—by being vulnerable, showing your true colors, throwing your judgments in the deep freeze, having the courage to truly listen and inquire—you will be beautifully prepared to meet another person (who's just as hungry for love as you are), and the love of your life will soon be banging down your door.

That's why, to be loved, be loving; it's that simple.

three

*T*rust

. . . .

Be patient toward all that is unsolved in your
heart and . . . try to love the questions
themselves. . . . Do not now seek the answers,
which cannot be given you because you would
not be able to live them. . . . Live the questions
now. Perhaps you will then gradually, without
noticing it, live . . . into the answer.

—Rainier Maria Rilke

. . . .

I have a trick I play when I'm going downtown to do an errand, and that's to "ask for a parking place." As I'm approaching the block where I need to be, I ask the beneficent spirits of parking and downtown clutter to prepare an empty space for me, so I can do my errand easily and quickly. It never fails. Whenever I "ask for" a parking place it magically appears. In fact, the other day when I asked for "a wonderful parking place," a grand, three-car limousine-sized space appeared directly outside the health food store. Trust is relying on this magic, and the experience of a happy outcome is the manifestation of our trust.

Trust is believing that the thing you had faith in will actually come to pass, and in a way more gracious and wonderful than you could have ever possibly imagined. It means that what you have believed in your heart, you can now rely on to become true in reality.

I often wonder if my parking trick really works or if it is just a "coincidence." But when I really pay attention, I discover that when I "ask for" a parking place it invariably appears, but if for even a moment I have so much as an eyelash of a doubt, I find that all the spaces are filled. That's because the magic only works if you *really* trust in it.

Trust is the living embodiment of faith. It is trust that allows us to believe that in a real moment in time, the thing that faith has allowed us to contemplate only in the abstract will actually come to pass. Trust is the comfort of being able to rest in the luminous conviction that things *will* occur exactly as we need them to, exactly as will be best for us.

Trust is gracious, motherly, and kind, a spiritual cradle to rest all our hopes in. Trust cares for us, for when we trust, we have put ourselves in the hands of what can actually occur. Trust is promise. Trust is the anticipation of joy. Trust is the star that will bring love to you.

6. *Be* Realistic About What Love Is

Trusting in love—that it will arrive, that it will be right and good for you—creates a comforting nest where you can rest your faith, so you can take the risk of taking a look at your hopes with a cool, clear eye. When you're being realistic—facing the truth about situations, people, and things—you're loving yourself. Instead of fooling yourself with out-of-reach expectations, you're taking care of yourself by asking for something that can actually come to pass.

Being realistic is a unique form of trust, because it asks that you be responsible. It asks you to use the left brain—intellect, awareness, evaluation—as well as the right—intuition, feeling, impulse—to protect you from just foolishly, irresponsibly falling into the kind of relationship that could be like taking a dive at the sidewalk.

To be realistic about love, you need to understand what a loving relationship is. A lot of people who are looking for love have such wildly unrealistic ideas that the relationships they imagine couldn't possibly occur. That's why they're constantly disappointed. They don't trust love and they shouldn't, because they're asking for the moon. But they also don't trust the real, wonderful suitors who could offer them a true experience of love.

Real love is both grand and simple. At its grandest, it contains all our most romantic ideals, and at its most elementary and gracious, it is the simple joy of having another person with whom to share life's journey. In the form of a an intimate relationship, love is both queenly and like a peasant girl, magnificent and very sweetly ordinary. It includes both the grand expanses of discovery and the ordinary pathways of daily life.

A relationship is the experience of trading feelings to a high degree, of being emotionally open and allowing another person's emotional reality to enter into yours, so there's an exchange through which you can both develop. It's the arena in which you can share your successes and woes, look for comfort and support, talk about the little irritating and huge overwhelming things that confront you day by day. It's the emotional connection that allows you to feel bonded to another human being, and because of this connection, also to become most yourself.

The greatest gift of an intimate relationship is that it can give you *you*. It's the opportunity to discover yourself in the presence of the reflecting emotions of another person: in the mirroring of another person's awareness and, at times, through his or her frustrating lack of awareness. It is in this intimate human context that you begin to discover what you really do feel, what's important to you, what delights you, what has troubled you always, and what's troubling you now.

Not all the things you discover are pleasant, but they are all great opportunities for growth. Growth and change are the fruits of love and this process of endlessly unfolding self-discovery is the greatest gift of any intimate relationship. As my personal trainer, Kerry, said when I asked him why he was so happy about being married: "It's an emotional workout; *I never stop growing.*"

Along with giving you yourself, a relationship is also a fine opportunity to apprehend another human being. It's a chance to really have the experience of knowing another person in the round—not according to your preconceptions, your dreams about who that person may be, all the needs of yours that he or she could fulfill, but of really discovering, as you might discover an incredibly beautiful landscape or an ancient sacred ruin, the mystery and beauty of another human being.

In this way, love teaches you what it is to be a human being, not only through your own feelings as they are endlessly evoked by your partner, but also through your experience of another person's uniqueness as it is endlessly revealed to you.

Being realistic about love doesn't mean that you "settle for less" or that there are compromises beyond bearing (although any relationship does require compromise). It means rather that you know love is graceful and gracious and will bring you many gifts—but not every single indulgence you could possibly imagine. Your relationship will be good to you, but it won't whisk you up out of your regular life and set you down in Fairyland. That's because love always gives us exactly what we need—nothing more and nothing less.

Real love can thrive only where realism is its waltz partner. That's because love won't solve all your problems and your relationship won't be a seamless, wrinkle-free union from the day you fall in love until the day death parts you from it. There's no Prince Charming; there's no perfect "10." You won't get everything you want, and you won't walk off hand in hand into the sunset while the credits roll.

Being realistic about love means understanding that love will always ask the best of you. Trusting in this will give you confidence in the capacity of love to change and enrich your life—even if it's in ways you never wished for or expected.

This is trust of the highest order, because at the level of our personalities, where we've been betrayed by parents, friends, and strangers, in little and huge ways, we want to trust only in the things that don't actually require trust: things that are surefire, fool proof, 100 percent guaranteed. In such situations of course, trust isn't necessary. There isn't any risk, and where there's no risk, trust is irrelevant.

Love, on the other hand, is full of risk, full of random possibilities and off-the-wall events. It's an experience that's constantly changing, creating itself moment by moment through hundreds of actions and interactions as we engage in it.

If you're willing to take the risk though, love *can* bring you incredible gifts: grand feelings, someone to wake up with in the morning, someone to cuddle up with at night, someone whose sorrows make your heart sad too, someone whose dreams you can happily share.

What Love Can Do

Love can make you feel good for a while, and if you tend it well, for a lifetime. It can give you a Friday night date, someone with whom to play Scrabble, a person to talk to about how your day was, someone to worry with over the income tax, someone to banish the feeling that you're all alone here on the planet. It can teach you about life's meaning; it can raise questions about your destiny. But it can't solve all your problems. It can't make up for every wound you suffered as a child, become the perfect mother or father you never had, or make your fears about whether you're really fulfilling your purpose all vanish like smoke in thin air.

Unfortunately, these are the very things we often ask love to do. We ask it to make up for every slight we ever experienced, to take away all our fears. We ask the person we love to stand up for us against any of the million possible difficulties life has to offer and make everything all right—and then blame him or her if things go wrong. No wonder so many relationships go awry!

Love can't be what I call an "existential umbrella"—an ever-protecting parasol that stands between you and everything bad that the heavens decide to dish out. Not only can't it be the answer to all your prayers, but it certainly doesn't mean that you can suddenly get lazy, as if as soon as you're in love, everything will be a piece of cake, and you don't have to lift a finger to create your own life anymore.

So many people who are alone have unrealistic expectations about love and believe that if only they could be in a relationship, all their troubles would be over. The emotional and spiritual error here is that when people make this assumption, they give up responsibility for their own lives and their own happiness.

Love can never take the place of personal responsibility and when we expect it to, we're asking for the impossible. In fact, when you make such unreasonable demands, love invariably doesn't show up—or doesn't last. It's almost as if the person coming toward you can feel the inappropriate purposes for which you have him or her in mind and is subtly instructed to move in a different direction. Why would anyone want to show up just to do the dirty work in your life? Love is a wonderful thing, a grand power, and the love gods aren't going to waste it on somebody who's not willing to do the work of building his or her own life.

When we expect love to do the impossible or imagine it's going to be an effortless undertaking, we're asking too much. Being realistic about love is trusting that it will give you what's truly appropriate for you, what is of value for your own growth and enhancement rather than all the things you think you want.

In the "what love can and can't do" department, I often think of Jean, a young woman I know who was madly searching for a mate and had dated a number of men, all of whom disappointed her. She was beginning to despair when, one day at a business lunch, she looked across the room to see a woman who was wearing a huge rock of a diamond ring. She looked at this woman all starry-eyed, as if she were the Queen of the World, because she had attained what, to Jean, was the unattainable: She'd found a rich man to marry her. After being stared at so long, the woman finally asked Jean, "Why are you staring at me? Have I offended you somehow or done something wrong?" At this, Jean, oddly overwhelmed, burst into tears and blubbered, "It's just that you're wearing such a beautiful diamond wedding set, you must be so terribly happy. I've been wanting to get married for ten years, but I can't find anyone to love me."

Then the woman looked at her and said, "You've got it all wrong; I have this ring *instead* of being happy. My husband gave me this ring and 'Will you marry me?' are about the last words he ever said. He'll never even have a conversation with me. He'd buy me five more wedding rings if I wanted, just to shut me up. In fact, I'm thinking of divorcing him. I wanted intimacy, but I got sidetracked by diamonds."

What Do You Really Want
Out of a Relationship?

Like the young woman in the story, it's easy to fantasize that "just being married" will make you happy and solve all your problems. This *if I just had a man, if I could just find a girlfriend, if I could only fall in love, then everything would be all right* kind of thinking falls into what I call the relationship daydreaming category.

Relationship daydreaming is the antithesis of relationship realism. Finding the love of your life is a sweet, serious undertaking, while relationship daydreaming is a kind of emotional sloppiness. Because fantasizing is vague and nonspecific, you won't get results. In love, as in anything else we ask for (a parking space, for example), *specificity brings results.* The cosmos can respond only when you send out a message loud and *clear.* If you need a new apartment, for example, you need to specify, I need a new apartment *in Cleveland.* Or, I need an apartment with *northern light so I can work on my paintings.* Or, *I need an apartment where the rent's no more than $500 a month—that's all my budget can handle.*

If you don't know precisely what you want, you won't get it. When it comes to falling in love, fuzziness of desire can cause you to drag out an unsatisfactory relationship, or to suffer by yourself so long that you miss out on the very relationship that might be perfect for you.

While a relationship isn't a panacea and certainly can't fulfill all your dreams, a good relationship does have certain characteristics, that can make it not only suitable, but truly wonderful for you. So let's get specific.

For starters, let's look at the activities you might like to enjoy with the person of your dreams. The reason this is so important is that, although you may not be thinking about it while you're feeling desperate, lonely, and miserable, when you *are* in a relationship, it will be comprised of all the things you either do or don't do with your partner. In their desperation to find someone to love, a lot of people overlook the vast areas of compatibility a relationship is actually made up of and try for unions with totally incompatible people.

The truth is, of course, that we all have a vast array of activities that are meaningful to us. Some are things we prefer to do on our own; others we like to share with someone. Bringing these two strands of preference into awareness is a major task of the realism of love, because often when we fall in love we mistakenly assume that we want or should want to share every moment and every experience with our partner, that "togetherness" is the only thing we desire.

If you make this mistake, it can often backfire later, as, within in the matrix of your relationship, you must once again discover the people, things, and experiences that nurture your individual spirit. In essence, we're all much more particular than the "whatever-he-likes, whatever-she-wants" state of mind; what's really important is the "what-you-want" state of mind.

Discovering Your Activity Preferences

Learning your own preferences will allow you to present yourself clearly and evaluate accurately the person who is presenting him or herself to you. Compatibility in terms of shared activities and alone/togetherness requirements are important components of any relationship. You can avoid a lot of missteps and disappointments, crossed wires and crabbiness if at the outset, you can communicate what your real preferences are.

So, as you're contemplating a relationship, let yourself become aware of all the things you like to do, both with a partner and by yourself. Make a list of *all* the things you like to do (for example, walk on the beach, make love, go to the movies, cook a gourmet dinner, go bungee jumping, hot air ballooning, or river rafting; do yoga, read a book, read twenty books, make beer, meditate, go to the gym).

Then beside each of the things on the list that you'd like to do with a sweetheart, put a "2" to indicate that these are things you like to do with someone and a put a "1" to express your preference for solitariness in a particular activity. Then put your list away for a week. When you look at it later with fresh eyes, what does it tell you about what you're looking for in a relationship? Your list will show you the activities you really do like to share and therefore the kind of relationship you'd prefer. It will also reveal the pockets of privacy you still want to preserve.

Of course, some of these things may change with time, or with a specific partner. You may have wanted to go dancing with someone in the past whereas you may not enjoy dancing with a particular partner now, because you'd rather go to art galleries with her—or you may be tired of dancing altogether.

In starting a relationship, don't ignore your list. It really is a reflection of who you are, and you can't abandon yourself completely for another person no matter how much "in love" you may feel. If your list says you like to go hiking *alone*—it's your meditation, your time for unwinding and communing with nature—and the woman you're dating says she wants to go hiking with you, in fact, that's the one thing she's always wanted to do with the man she's related to, then you've got a problem. Maybe it's a problem that can be negotiated, but it's certainly one that needs to be addressed.

If you're the world's coldest person who wears bedsocks even in the tropics, and the man who's courting you wants to spend his whole life on the ski slopes with the woman of his dreams, then, ditto, you also have a problem. If your list says you love to socialize, to do business with a vivacious woman at your side, and the woman you're dating is a bookworm who doesn't even own a black dress, you've got a Grand Canyon of discrepancies to handle.

Conversely, if you like to work in the garden with someone and he does too, if you like to raise flowers and she loves to arrange them, if you both love to go sailing or shopping in Paris, then you're in the happy land of some instant compatibilities.

Your list can also show you how much of a relational person you are. Are you a lose-yourself-in-a-relationship kind of guy or do you like to keep some privacy for yourself? If you have ten things on your list, and you'd like to share them all, then maybe you need to add a few more that are just for you by yourself. It's not healthy to drown with somebody else, no matter how much in love you are. Every list should have a few items of solitude on it—we all need time for personal rejuvenation. On the other hand, if you have ten things on your list and only one or two are things you'd like to do with somebody else, maybe you're really a loner who doesn't want a full-time relationship.

Of course, it's also important to realize that, as a relationship goes on, it often develops new energy, which can shift the focus of what you like to do together or alone. The birth of a child can do that; so can changed financial circumstances that allow for travel, or the purchase of a house, which can bring out individual or joint fix-it-up tendencies. One of the things you enjoyed doing alone in the past (for example, working out at the gym, or cooking) may be something you'd now like to share with your partner and can become a new way for you both to grow together.

Whatever your relationship activity preferences are, it's important to identify them now, keep them in mind while you're choosing a partner, and realize that with time and the effects of the partnership itself, they will probably change.

The S.Q.N. of Love

Realism about love also means that, along with knowing your activity preferences, you're aware of the one thing that the person you're looking for absolutely must have. This is what I call the *sine qua non* (S.Q.N.) of a relationship.

Sine qua non is a Latin phrase that means "without which not." As I apply it to relationships, it means the thing *without which* the relationship would *not* exist. We all have something that's an absolutely indelible, uncompromisable requirement when it comes to choosing another human being to love. It may be positive, something they must have—that they're emotionally conscious, that they're willing to communicate, that they share your belief in God. Or it may be a negative requirement, something they absolutely must not do, be, or have; for example, that they really don't want to have children, don't use drugs, or don't want to have a conventional relationship.

Whatever it is, your S.Q.N. is the thing without which

you really cannot fall in love, and the thing that your partner must also hold in equal value. This is where relationships either flourish or falter, because the S.Q.N. represents a core value for both partners, and it must continue to be held in common for the relationship to endure.

The S.Q.N. is the grounding bond that, over time, allows the various imperfections of your relationship to recede, the thing that forms the strong armature on which the structure of your love is developed as the years go by. Conversely, if it doesn't exist in common, as with the diamond-ring lady who ignored her own S.Q.N.—emotional intimacy—in time it will become the reason for a potential breakup.

The reason the S.Q.N. is so important is because in any given relationship, you really can't get everything you want from another person, and they can't from you, either. That's why it's essential to make sure you both get your S.Q.N., because you will feel totally shortchanged if you get a handful of your preferences, but not the one thing that fulfills your deepest need.

It's often the S.Q.N. that's operating when you see a couple and wonder, What do those two see in one another? For example, I once knew a highbrow publishing executive who was married to a Hell's Angel. From all outward appearances, they were a mismatch. But at the level of their S.Q.N., they were a perfect pair: they both loved motorcycles and, after having difficult lives, were each looking for a partner to play with. Another "odd" couple, a doctor and her handyman husband, have as their S.Q.N. the joint commitment to live their relationship as a conscious emotional process. Never underestimate the power of the S.Q.N. as a relationship creator; it is responsible for the oddest—and happiest—pairings.

As your life unfolds, your S.Q.N. may shift. When you're young, your absolute necessity may be a partner who wants to have children; when you're middle-aged, it may be a person who shares your spiritual values. But no matter what your age, no matter at what point you are in your own development, if you're looking for love, you need to know what your S.Q.N. is now.

The realism here lies in facing the fact that the thing you won't compromise is not a fantasy but an absolute necessity for you. It means being aware, for example, that even if he's the tallest, handsomest, most gorgeous hunk of a guy, who's got a great sense of humor, but is a high-powered executive who works 14 hours a day, and your S.Q.N. is that the person you love be able to spend quiet evenings at home with you, no amount of good looks or great jokes will make him an acceptable partner.

In addition to the S.Q.N., we all have a number of things we'd *prefer* to have in a relationship. For example, you'd like a person who's healthy, not an insomniac (a bed-wrecker, as I call it), who has a good sense of aesthetics and likes going to the movies. Or you'd like a man who's taller than you, who's a vegetarian, likes to travel, and is a good conversationalist. Or you'd like a woman who has red hair, enjoys skiing, is a reader, and laughs at your jokes.

This is the stuff of personals ads, desires that, if you really want to have a relationship, you should be willing to compromise or negotiate about. For example, I'd *like* a redhead, but she's an adorable brunette; I'd *rather* he be taller than I am, but he isn't, and really, it's fine. Relationships—and people—never come with exactly the attributes we'd like, and everything except your S.Q.N. should be open to revision.

Give yourself a break, though, by getting to know your preferences before you start. They will help you understand the kind of partner you want and maximize the possibility of finding someone appropriate. Otherwise you might end up marrying a giraffe, when you were really looking for a zebra.

Here's a little quiz to help you figure this out. Take a few minutes now to reflect on your essential requirement and preferences in a mate:

- What is your relationship S.Q.N.—the one thing you really cannot live without?

- What are your lesser relationship preferences? List as many as you can think of. Which of these are negotiable?

- And, just for fun, what attributes or experiences would you be happy to be surprised by?

Is This the One?

In the dating game, people can spend an incredibly long time trying to figure out if the person who shows up is "the one," or, as I like to say, whether he or she is "the real turtle soup or merely the mock." Being able to recognize "the one" doesn't have to do with whether he or she showed up with the right props—46 diamonds or a big fancy car.

Rather, it has to do with your capacity for self-aware ness, as well as your ability to assess another person accurately. This awareness of self and others refers to your knowing your activity preferences, your S.Q.N., your negotiable desires and also understanding these for another person.

But this assessment of yourself and another will take you only so far. For these characteristics exist at the level of personality, and we are also spiritual beings. We have morals, values, and an inner intuitive sense of the meaningfulness of our lives. So therefore, when you're choosing "the one," these deeper levels of your being will also be operating. Your soul as well as your personality will have to be satisfied by your choice.

At the soul level, the person you fall in love with should reflect and support your values. Sometimes in the heat of passionate romance or the desperation of loneliness, it's easy to ignore this. You just want to fall in love; you're not thinking about your politics, your commitment to saving the environment; your belief in family loyalty, or that you're an unflinching stickler for honesty. But in the long run, these things do count, and can be either the source of shared commitments or the downfall of your relationship. So take a moment to reflect on those values:

- What's the most important thing in your life: Your health? Your sobriety? Creativity? Spiritual life? Your children? Leaving something that heals the world? Kindness? Being a contributor instead of a user? Saving the planet?

- What are you willing to stake your life on—or give it up for? (This will show you a lot about where your deepest values are.)

Whatever these values are, they represent a position you've taken as a person, not just for a moment, but most likely for a lifetime. They also say something about your life's path—what you're doing here on earth—and although you may not need your partner to feel as passionate about your values as you do, you will need the person you love to honor and respect you for holding your position.

Once you've been truthful about your values, perhaps you'll see that the person you fell in love with last Friday night isn't, in fact, the person with whom you'd like to spend the rest of your life. You've discovered, based on your realistic assessment, that you can enjoy the interlude, and, when it's appropriate, come to the moment of departure. If that's the case with you, enjoy the relationship while you can; let go of it when you must, and, if necessary, be willing to be lonely a little while longer.

Trust Your Instincts

If you discover that the person you're exploring having a relationship with is, in some graphic way, not the right person, don't be afraid to change your mind. One of the greatest discoveries in the process of falling in love is finding out that you really can trust your instincts. If the man you have a wild crush on shows up to your first date wearing chartreuse high heels (as one woman's first date did), it might just be that he'd really prefer to have a boyfriend (as this woman's suitor eventually did). If your instincts tell you that something feels wrong, don't be afraid to act on them.

If you've caught the wrong fish—it's undersized or out of season—enjoy it, look at all its beautiful attributes, its shiny scales, its iridescent eyes, but be willing to throw it back into the pond. Remember, it's all right to be alone for a little while longer; in fact, one's own aloneness can be a great teacher and the source of further preparation for the love you really deserve.

7. Recognize the Higher Purpose of a Relationship

We are all in the beautiful, endlessly unfolding process of our own development. We're not tin soldiers or nutcracker humans; we are living beings who are a pliable, changeable, fluid, self-creating consciousness that is being formed and reformed as we live our lives through the individuals and circumstances we encounter.

That's why every relationship you have, no matter how short, is purposeful. It is a transformational process of two souls' evolution and mutual psychological healing. To the degree that you're conscious of this deep purpose, you become able both to recognize the love that's right for you and to also receive its benefits.

The truth is that when you call love into your life, you're asking for a very great thing. You're asking not only for someone who meets your relationship requirements as you explored them in Chapter 6, but also that you step into alignment with your life's highest purpose.

For whether you are consciously aware of it or not, the person who joins you in love is really stepping into your life to fulfill that purpose. Whether his or her role is great or small in relation to the magnitude of your life's journey, whether he or she joins you by bringing joy or the frustrations that refine and ultimately define you, this person is arriving to join you in your purpose. The same is true for you *vis-à-vis* him or her. You have entered the other person's life to fulfill some high purpose of his or hers, and the dance of those two purposes is the sacred tango of love.

When you step into an awareness of this high purposefulness, you can immediately trust that the person who is being sent to you comes to you to assist in the fulfilling of your purpose, even if this is only a teaching interlude and not the longstanding love of your life.

Your Life Purpose

For many of us, our own sense of purpose is only vaguely comprehended. "A purpose?" you may say. "My purpose is to get up and go to work so I can pay the rent and have a little time to myself somewhere along the line." We tend to think of our purpose in the limited framework of survival, of getting from one day to the next.

But in each of us there's the seedling of a grand purpose, and our spiritual path is to heighten and develop our awareness of that tender plant. This means looking inward and asking, What am I doing here? What has my life been leading to? Why have I been given the opportunity to exist as a human being of this gender, with these particular attributes, going through the unique set of experiences that I'm going through?

We were all born with a very specific purpose to fulfill,

not randomly dropped off on the planet just to take up space and assist in the destruction of the environment. The more you are consciously aware of what your function is, the more clear you will be about who your true partner is for the journey.

Your purpose can be most difficult to see during times of upheaval or tragedy, when life can seem random, cruel, and purposeless. Yet it is often in these moments, when life seems most mysterious and bleak, that a true life's destiny emerges—the woman suffering from a life threatening illness discovers a healing process that saves hundreds of lives; the man who loses his wife in a plane crash becomes a grief counselor; the woman unable to bear children becomes a fertility expert. Suddenly a life's purpose is made visible, and we step into alignment with it.

Fortunately, most of us don't have to suffer so extremely to find our life's purpose, and that's why intimate relationships are so important. For, more than anything else we do, they help focus and develop this purposefulness in our lives. They can deliver us to our purpose, heal us from whatever stands in the way of fulfilling it, or be the partnerships that embody the enactment of it.

The historians Will and Ariel Durant are such an example, as are Madame Curie and her husband. Any romantic relationship can be a partnership at whose core is the fulfillment of a purpose larger than the relationship itself—whether that purpose is rearing children, creating a business, or starting a university, to name but a few.

So take a look at what your life's purpose might be:

- As far as you can tell at this moment, what is your life's purpose? What are you here for? To serve or teach? To be an artist, musician, or writer? To create or assist those who create? To be a brilliant businessperson? Are you here to be a statesman or a leader? Illumined parent? Philosopher or healer?

When you fall in love through the window of awareness that your life has a purpose, the quality of love that can come to you becomes immediately much higher than if you're simply looking from the point of view of "I'm bored, I wish someone would come along to amuse me." You're asking for the highest quality of love you could possibly entertain, because where there's great love there is also great purpose; and where there's great purpose, there's also the opportunity for a great love.

Recognizing the essential purposefulness of our relationships allows us to see their great beauty. More than anything else, our relationships teach us that we are constantly in a process of becoming. We are endlessly unfolding as human beings-in-relationship, from the moment of our birth, as we enter a family and are subjected to the constellation of experiences that constitute our life themes. We then begin the long journey of living out the variations on that theme as they are expressed in school, with brothers and sisters, with peers and colleagues, in society and at work. All that we are and become is delivered to us in some form of relationship.

Whether or not you can see clearly from your past relationships the path on which they have been taking you, your history of relationships has indeed been bringing you toward your life's destination. Believing this can, at times, require trust. To know in your heart that no matter how frustrating or disappointing your past relationships may have been, each of them helped shape your life's purpose—that is a great act of trust. When you accept this profound truth, your life will become more graceful, and the relationship that is exactly right for you now will have a chance to come into being.

Our Developmental Tasks

We each have a life body of relationships, a lineage that traces our own developmental process, both as personalities and as souls. Our intimate relationships serve as the medium by which we go through a series of growth processes—psychological changes that enable us to become fully formed human beings, and spiritual changes that enhance the brilliance of our souls. The degree to which we achieve the epitome of what it is to be a well-balanced and spiritually vital person, of course, depends on how willing we are to go through the transformations that our relationships offer.

On the personality level, we're just trying to keep moving through the alphabet of our own personal evolution. We do this by engaging in a series of growth processes I call our "developmental tasks." Through them, we gradually resolve the questions originally posed by the life's theme you were introduced to in Chapter 3.

Whenever we establish relationships, we intuitively seek the partners who can help us undertake these developmental tasks in order to unravel the meanings, heal the wounds, and transcend the limitations generated by our childhoods. Some of these tasks are external and have to do with completing incomplete parenting. In such instances, your partner may be helping you develop skills, attitudes, and behaviors that weren't nurtured or fostered in you.

Other developmental tasks have to do with your emotional healing. This means that in one form or another, through your intimate relationship, you will relive and resolve the painful life theme of your childhood, either by reencountering some aspect of it, or by discovering that there's an alternative to it. Whatever your particular theme, you are intuitively trying to resolve it, and every relationship that comes into your life is playing a role in that resolution as you steadily move toward emotional wholeness.

The actual accomplishing of these developmental tasks may be completely invisible in a relationship, but whether we are consciously aware of it or not, we are always doing this. You may not be thinking to yourself, I've picked a married woman who isn't really available, with whom to have my intimate relationship so I can relive the abandonment I felt when I was ten and my mother died. But if this is your issue and your current situation, chances are this *is* what you are trying to work out.

Or you probably aren't thinking, Here I am in a relationship with a person who's a critical self-righteous egotist just like my father, so I can finally feel the rage I never felt at him. But the truth is, whether you cotton to what's going on or not, it *is* going on. That's the beauty and the power of an intimate relationship—it's always bringing up these themes and always offering an opportunity for their resolution.

At times, these tasks may be obvious: we're trying to learn a skill or change a habit—finishing a college degree, for example, or learning how to manage money. Or they may be more subtle and interior: finding the partner who can help you to connect with your self-confidence; coming to terms with the beauty of your body; helping you believe that in spite of being beaten yourself, you can become a wonderful father.

For each of us, it's important to look at what our developmental tasks are and how they solve our psychological issues; otherwise, we tend to just blindly repeat them. I'm reminded here of a woman named Anne who desperately wanted to be a sculptor, and consecutively married four addicts: an alcoholic, a drug abuser, a gambler, and a food addict. In her case, four—not three—was a charm. It was only after the fourth shocking marriage came to an end that she thought, "Hmm, this must be an issue in *my* life. I wonder what I'm trying to resolve here, because I keep falling in love with addicts?"

When Anne finally got into therapy, she saw that she had deep unresolved issues about both her father and mother. Her mother had been a food addict; her father an alcoholic. She had incredible rage at both of them that she had never dealt with.

In dealing with her pain—a long process with much rage and many tears—she became gradually able to establish relationships with men where, instead of simply repeating this pattern, she could give and receive love that was healthy, accepting, and kind. In her case, the repetition of this pattern and the subsequent awakening it provoked both resolved her personality issues and brought her soul to a place where she could claim her own creativity and become the powerful sculptor she now is.

Each of us has a lineage of relationships. Like Anne, some of them are "bad" experiences, unpleasant to remember, where the gift comes through an awakening from the repetition of past unresolved pain. Others have been granted us to provide an experience of something wonderful we never had before: a man to hold you tenderly; a woman to listen empathetically when you're expressing your feelings.

Whenever I speak of these developmental tasks, people often remark that they seem to embody a very unromantic view of love; it's like doing an autopsy on a relationship. Instead of looking at its captivating beauty, we look at the bones, muscles, and heartbeat that sustain it.

The truth is that while this may seem momentarily unromantic, the minute we look at our relationships this way and start honoring them as fulfilling this evolutionary purpose, we appreciate them on an entirely new level. Rather than seeing the people we have loved as a bunch of random folks who just showed up in our lives, we recognize them as healers, helpers, magicians, knights in shining armor, queens, and majesties. We see that all we have done with them and they with us has moved us along the path of our own highest development.

I was speaking to a woman the other day who said, "I had a most difficult marriage, but it taught me unconditional love—what an incredible gift." A divorced man who's begun to see his relationship life in this way, realized that, while he hadn't found the happiness he desired with his wife, she had given him two beautiful children. Through them, he had learned the joys of parental love, and had finally become able to forgive his own extremely abusive mother.

Your Life Body of Relationships

We're all traveling to the place in our hearts and souls where we can live in the state of grace that is love. But each of us is in a different place on that journey. Because love *is* a journey, it behooves you to be aware of which hotel or road sign you've stopped at, to see where you are and where you need to go next. So, as you're poised at this particular moment, preparing yourself for someone new to arrive, it would be good to review your heritage of relationships in light of your developmental tasks.

Take a look at the constellation of people who've stepped into your life to be your high-school sweetheart, summer lover, first husband or wife, live-in love partner, or wretched, pain-in-the-butt-relationship failure, and see how each of these has assisted you on your path.

To do this, I suggest that you write "The Relationship Review." This exercise is like taking a walk through the formal gardens of your love life, stopping to take note of those people (some of them may be statues now, concrete and encrusted) who have stood in your midst and played a role in your heart.

- Write the names of all the significant love relationships in your life—beginning with your first love. Next to each name, write a little about what your relationship was like:

- What was its hallmark experience? (e.g., the trip to Europe; building a house together; the birth of your child.)

- If you had to sum up the essence of your relationship in one phrase like a movie title, what would you call it? (e.g.: Two Ships Passing in the Night; Too Little, Too Late; A Summer in Paradise; All Work and No Play.)

- How did you change during this relationship?

- How are you different now because of having been in it?

- If you were to say a heartfelt thank you to this person for what you got out of the relationship, what would you say? (e.g., "Thank you for helping me launch the business"; "Thank you for showing me what I need to avoid.")

- Finally, as you look at your own progression of relationships, let yourself see what your developmental task with each person was. Do you see that your relationship journey has been one primarily of healing your childhood wounds? Of nurturing the talent that is your gift to the world? Of developing your sense of the sacredness of life? Getting organized? Growing up? Moving from fear to love?

You may observe as you review your relationships that they seem to have followed a very scattered pattern. In one, perhaps you were discovering the capabilities of your mind. In another, you may have focused on your body—getting fit, changing your eating habits, giving up an addiction, recognizing that indeed your body is the house of your spirit. Some relationships are playful; some speak to your need for healing; others advance the work of your soul. All have been necessary to your evolution. Whether you are now ready for a playmate, a soul mate, or a housemate, each relationship you've had has played a few notes in the sonata of your life.

As you complete your Relationship Review, hopefully you will begin to realize that you can trust your soul's wisdom. Every relationship is a journey on both a personality and soul level. Since we spend so much time in our personalities—where we feel pain and delight, longing and attachment, happiness and misery—we often feel our personalities are who we are. But behind the scenes, our souls are always working, creating the experiences that will ensure a higher level of evolution where we not only "feel good" but, more importantly, fulfill our life's true purpose.

As you review the history of your intimate relationships, you can get a glimpse of your soul's work. You will see again and again that while what you may have expected didn't quite come to pass, something else important did. You grew in ways you couldn't have imagined, changed in ways you had never dreamed of. Above all, you see that there was always a plan operating on your behalf, and that, by moving through the progression of your relationships, you have come closer and closer to fulfilling your life's unique purpose.

It's time to leave the past and discover what your soul and personality are asking love to bring you now. For whatever that is, it is your new developmental task, and the person you are waiting for is the person who will help you accomplish it. For whatever your current developmental task may be—for example, to have a baby, to learn to be more feminine, to have fun, to feel blissful love—it is precisely this task that the person you're going to fall in love with now will help you undertake.

8. Apprehend Your Soul's Wisdom in Creating a New Relationship

Writing the Relationship Review should give you a sense of optimism about the future. For hopefully you have seen that no matter how the person of your dreams comes to you—strangely, out of nowhere, or as part of the ordinary course of your life—he or she is part of the grand plan that has been held in store for you since the beginning of time. Whether you meet your love on a street corner or select him or her from hundreds of candidates on display at the video dating service, this person is a gift from the cosmos to help with whatever issue is "up" for you right now.

This moment of the conjunction of what you have already completed in your past relationships and what you need to undertake next is "The Window of Possibility." It is a moment of great opportunity for change, a pivotal point at which you're poised to take the next step.

Because you're reading this book, it's most likely that in your life, there's a vacancy of love you want to fill. This void or open space is one of the hallmarks of a Window of Possibility. Windows of Possibility contain the vacancies that are the necessary conditions of creating change. In the twelve-step programs, for example, they speak of "hitting bottom." The "bottom" is the black hole in which all possibilities of receiving pleasure from an addiction have finally been exhausted; from this void a person can be reborn.

Just as birth itself comes from a dark void, so every step of our own life change comes from the well of emptiness.

Windows of Possibility are created by crises or losses, emptinesses or completions. If you suddenly have a serious illness, for example, there's hole in your usual experience that makes you open to change. If you end a relationship, there's room for a new one to come in; if you lose a friend, you have time for a new friend; if you experience a great loss because of a business failure, there's an opportunity for deep self-examination.

Windows of Possibility are moments of awakening, intervals in which changes you've wanted to make, but haven't quite been able to, suddenly become possible. The precipitating event of your Window of Possibility may be very obvious. You may be ending a long career or you may have just moved to a new city; you may have finally left your parents' house and gone away to college; finished raising your two children alone; been widowed, or spent your tenth year of lonely nights at home without a relationship. Each of these creates a juncture at which you're ready to partake of something new—a person or a set of experiences that will help you move further down the path of your individual evolution.

Whether we recognize it or not, life is a series of Windows of Possibility that pinpoint turning points of major change. The very fact you're consciously seeking a relationship is a Window of Possibility for you. And the more you can be aware of this window and the specifics of your current developmental task, the more you'll be able to recognize the perfect person when he or she arrives. Aha, you'll say, here's the person who's been sent to help me open my heart, to assist me with the transition from being a widow to a lover, from being a career-focused person to a man who's emotionally awake.

Take a few moments now to identify what created your own Window of Possibility and your new developmental task:

- What is the process you have just completed? (For example, I just broke up with my boyfriend; I just finished the work on my Ph.D.; my kids just went off to college.)

- What is the opening that has been created? (More time? More freedom? More self-awareness?)

- What, as far as you can tell, is your next developmental task? In other words, what is the thing you are most seeking to develop or change in your life right now? Is it resolving a conflict with one of your parents or siblings? Solving a negative relationship with money? Getting over your fear of success? Your inability to trust? Learning to get angry? To receive?

As you can see, understanding your current developmental task is one way of discovering what you need out of a relationship. For what you need out of the relationship you're currently seeking is what hasn't been addressed by any of your previous relationships. It could be anything: a truly satisfying sexual connection that seems to have eluded you all your life; the daily comforting companionship of a partner who quietly cares about you; the children you've dreamed of having but postponed because of your career; the sharing of a career; the joy of intellectual stimulation; the opportunity to be nurtured and supported in your creativity; the pleasure and security of sharing a household.

As you can see, there are many levels to your development, which run from very basic to sublime. You may be standing tiptoe at the brink of spiritual enlightenment or you may have some simple, yet meaningful, needs you'd like to have met by an intimate relationship. Where you are is where you are—no value judgments. Your personality and soul are both steadfast in the process of your evolution, and all you have to do is make yourself available to the person who will be right for you.

Don't be surprised if the thing you need now is completely different from what you wanted when you were eighteen or what it will be when you're eighty. Remember, you have a right to need exactly what you need at this moment; you have a right, in the divine generosity of love, to have your heart's desire fulfilled.

Whatever your next task is, keep it in mind as the thing you really do need now. Because through your soul's care the person you need to assist you, to be your companion in that process, will certainly be brought to you.

· · · · · · ·

When I speak to people about becoming consciously aware of what they need from love, they often express embarrassment: "Oh my goodness, can I really ask for this—to finally have self-confidence, to feel beautiful, to be financially secure. It's as if it were somehow shameful to actually *want* to get something out of love. It's almost as if we've been trained to just take love as it comes, to keep our specific hopes under wraps, and not to realize that these hopes in themselves are part of the way we move down our life's path.

A few years ago I met a young woman who had grown up in abject poverty—her family of six had lived in a chicken coop. In spite of almost no encouragement, she had managed to finish high school, get quite a good job, and move into an apartment of her own. In talking about the relationship she hoped for, she said, "This may sound shallow, but I could really fall in love with just about any man who could provide for me. If I could stop feeling poor, I would really feel loved."

I ran into this woman recently and she had met such a man. "I'm grateful every day," she said, "He loves me, and he's a wonderful provider. We have two small children now, and because of the security I feel, I'm really able to love them in a way I never could have if I were scared about money all the time."

Some of us are embarrassed about wanting someone who can make us feel handsome or beautiful—or smart, or funny, or talented—or about needing someone who will love us in spite of our own naked needs and real limitations. Whatever your particular need for love is right now, honor it deeply. Your soul will be satisfied only when this particular longing has been fulfilled. For your longing is your soul's deep wisdom; it will always bring you the experience that will keep you on your soul's highest path.

A Wish List for Your Perfect Mate

Telling yourself exactly what you'd like in your perfect mate is part of what will conjure this person into being. While some of the items on your list may seem superficial, they actually represent the way your soul's wisdom is operating in the real world, and being specific helps your soul do its work of bringing the right love to you.

All of us envision in one form or another. We daydream. We talk about falling in love with our friends; we fantasize when someone who's got some of the attributes we want catches our eye at the grocery store or shows up across the room at a party. But vague wishes aren't enough; you need to define exactly what sort of person could fill your falling in love bill, or the great "supermarket in the sky" won't know who to send.

It's amazing how people do get what they ask for. One woman I know confessed she'd spent her whole life falling in love with handsome hunks, and after divorcing a hunk (a one-and-a-half-year marriage) and being alone for five years, she finally put on her refrigerator half a dozen pictures of what she called, "regular, good men." "I finally realized that I wanted to be loved," she said, "and that I'd be happy being loved by an ordinary man who would love me back."

Within about a month, friends invited her to a dinner party where she met a man who was a little shorter than she, losing his hair, and, the sweetest person she'd ever met. She said it was like finding the man she'd been looking for in all those gorgeous hunks—she'd just been confused about the packaging. Not long after they started living together, and they've been happily together for nine years.

The photos on the fridge were this woman's wish list. As for your own, maybe you'd like to create a collage like she did, or write your requirements on a sheet of lace-edged pink paper and tuck it in your lingerie drawer, or just hold it as a vision. One woman told me that when she wanted to fall in love, she kept shutting her eyes until finally she "saw" a man come into view.

"I couldn't quite believe it," she told me later, "but one day when I squeezed my eyes shut, there he was, walking back and forth in front of a boutique. Every time I thought about wanting to fall in love, I'd just close my eyes, and there he'd be again, walking back and forth in front of that store. I thought it was weird, but I just kept trusting and closing my eyes. Six months after I started having my vision, I met my husband at a political mixer. You guessed it. He's the owner of the boutique."

Whether you choose to envision, ask, or perform a ceremony to conjure up the person of your dreams, it's good, at some point, to make a specific list. The first item on the list, of course, should be your S.Q.N. and also don't forget to ask that the person be able to bring something to the developmental task you've just identified.

But don't stop there. Paint as complete a picture as you can: that she lives in the same town; that she loves music; would like to have children; has blonde hair and brown eyes; that he's not now or never has been an alcoholic; that he's tall, communicative, a good lover; that he doesn't watch football; that he has a driver's license. (I know one woman in her late 30s who had never dated a man who had a driver's license. When she was making her list, that was the first thing that came up. She ended up marrying a very successful man, but when he sent for her in a limousine on their first date, the first thing she asked him was "You do have a driver's license, don't you?")

It's important to make your list both thorough and specific, to include both whatever big and little odd things are imperative for you. Just as when you're shopping, you don't say, "I want a black dress," you say, "I want a black dress with three-quarter-length sleeves, a portrait neckline, a patent leather belt, and a flared skirt," when you're making a love list, you don't just say "I want a man."

Don't ask for the moon—"I want him to be a millionaire who'll take me to Zanzibar" or "I want her to be a clone of Marilyn Monroe"—but do ask for the things that are really important to you, the things that will nurture you, make you feel strong, secure, challenged—and loved. Be *very* specific, because words are the architecture of reality, and the universe will respond very specifically to your request.

In fact, you may be shocked to discover how specific the answer might be. I know a divorcee who made this list, because she'd decided she wanted to get married. Her list said, "I want the man who shows up to be intelligent, successful, rich, appreciate me, take me to nice dinners, be culturally stimulating, encourage me with my work, and accept my children." She even added as a postscript, "I don't mind if he's been married before or has children of his own." She had a very comprehensive list; she filed it in her computer and put it out of her mind.

Within a few weeks, a man did show up in her life. He fit to the T each one of her wish list attributes. He had money, was successful, took her to movies and the theater, really appreciated who she was, and in the twinkling of an eye helped her start her own business. He had been married before and was willing to accept her children—but the kicker was that he absolutely did not want to get married again. She'd forgotten to ask for her most important item!

So what are the things you'd like from your ideal mate? Make a list of at least 15 things that you'd like to be true about the person you're calling into your life. Then, put it away somewhere and let it do its magic.

Your Soul Knows the Timing

As you can see from looking at all that's already happened to you, your life hasn't been a hapless adventure of random circumstances, but rather a soul adventure that's more like a tapestry whose pattern has beauty and meaning. Now, as a further act of trust, you need to start really believing that, along with everything else, your soul knows the right timing for your next relationship.

I'm sure you've had experiences in your life where you wanted something (a beautiful white wool jacket, for example), couldn't get it when you wanted it (you couldn't afford it), and gave up, only to find out that the delay had been for a reason (the white jacket went on sale three weeks later, and you got it for half price).

The same is true for true love. It may look like it will never arrive, but you have to trust that the wait is for a good reason.

I met a lovely couple at a wedding recently. They were both in their 50s and had been married just a few years. When I asked the man how they'd met, he said, "Oh, I've known her for 25 years. I was madly in love with her in college, but she wouldn't even date me. She was already smitten with the guy she eventually married. I didn't run across her again until after her divorce. I'm so glad we didn't get together when we were young; we would have destroyed each other. We've both had enough experience now to know how lucky we are."

Trusting the timing means that somewhere deep inside, you know it will take just as long as it takes, no shorter or longer. It's recognizing that the timing's out of your hands. In a sense, it's out of your control when the love of your life is going to show up. The timing is dependent on so many factors—your mutual availability, your awareness of your life theme and emotional makeup, your developmental tasks, and your capacity to love. All of these must combine to create a relationship that is a true conjunction of both of your needs and spirits.

Just as this man said it would have been a disaster if he and his wife had tried to fall in love before, so it is with each successful relationship—there's always the matter of timing. I know a couple, both married for the first time in their forties, who recognized that only now were they ready to be married. John had spent most of his youth smoking pot. In his late 30s, he finally got sober, dealt with the emotional issues he'd been avoiding by being stoned all those years, built a career, and realized that he was ready to risk falling in love. John's developmental task was learning the skills of love in an intimate relationship.

Simone, on the other hand, had been abandoned by her father, who was so busy working that he never had time for her. She'd spent her 20s and 30s being so caught up with her career (trying to get her father's love by being exactly like him), that, as she said, she wouldn't have been available for love anyway. Now, at 40, with her business established and the issue of her father's rejection somewhat resolved, she was ready to fall in love and have a baby. John and Simone both agreed that they wouldn't have given each other so much as the time of day before the moment they met.

As their story shows, there are always invisible factors operating in the background, little kinks that need to be ironed out, riddles that need to be solved. You can never be sure of the preparations your soul is asking you to complete before love will show its face. You can't hurry love, but if you trust your soul's wisdom, you can wait patiently (instead of desperately or hopelessly), knowing that when the timing is right, your person to love will appear.

So, whatever your fears, whatever impatience you carry in your back pocket, whatever your roster of expectations about how, who, and when, the universe has a surprise for you. There are only two requirements: one, that you know you want to be loved, and two, that you trust your soul to know when to bring love to you. It will always be perfect; for, when the person you love arrives, he or she will be a stitch in the great design, not only of *your* life, but of both your lives' intersecting.

four

$\mathcal{S}$urrender

. . . .

The winds of grace are blowing all the time —
it is up to us to raise the sail.

—Ramakrishna

. . . .

*S*urrender is a beautiful movement in which you gracefully, willingly, languidly fall, only to find midway that you have been gathered into some unimaginable embrace. Surrender is letting go, whether or not you believe the embrace will occur. It's trust to the hundredth power—not sticking to your idea of the outcome, but letting go in the faith that even the absence of an outcome will be the perfect solution.

Surrender is diaphanous and fluid. It's the giving up of rigidity of every kind: rigidities of the mind that design outcomes to occur in very specific ways; rigidities of the heart that refuse the heart to be soft and open; rigidities of the body that refuse to receive the touch that could heal, the passion that could transform; rigidities of the soul that congeal and congest the spirit, causing it to imagine it has a life apart from the body and mind.

Surrender is meltdown of every rigidity we've ever been committed to, the conscious and unconscious dismantling of how we thought things should be to make way for the way things will, in fact, occur. It's a kind of being surprised by joy, of happily swimming into the greater consciousness that's always operating on our behalf. Just as a child, learning to swim, discovers, amazed, that the water does hold him up, so surrender buoys us up, supports us for the fulfillment of our destinies.

Surrender requires purity of intention. In the absolute freedom it grants in response to our letting go, it requires an absolute commitment of holding on to nothing. Whatever you thought you had—the idea, the expectation, the plan, the hope of how things should be—you must let go of it fully. Surrender is stepping away from the certainty of your categories into the no-man's-land of all possibilities.

And it is in surrendering, in letting go into the void—into the mysterious, unnamed, mystical, formless future; into the arms that are invisible—that we become finally ready to receive it all. Surrender is the giving of your all to the All; the waiting with an absolute absence of expectation for the totally perfect thing to occur.

9. Embrace the Paradox of Love

True love is paradoxical: Everything you can say about it is both true and not true at the same time. This applies to the nature of love itself—that it is exalted *and* mundane; that it takes us to limitless joy, but also has its limitations; that it fulfills our demands to be loved, while totally defying and ignoring our specific requirements.

The way this paradox manifests in the real world is that if you insist on something about love, you never get it—or you do. If you insist that it arrives at a certain time, comes in a certain package, lasts a certain length of time, behaves in a certain way, challenges you in exactly all the ways you'd like it to, you'll never get it—or, on the other hand, you'll get exactly what you ordered.

You just never know. That's the paradox of love. As someone said to a dear friend of mine as she stood devastated after the breakup of her fourteen-year-marriage, "Well, maybe now the man of your dreams will come along and you'll live happily ever after, or maybe you'll be miserable for the rest of your life." In her case, amazingly, she found the perfect man six months later, but of course there was no guarantee that she would.

The paradoxes embedded in love reveal the great truth that love is always a gift. We can want it, ask for it, pray for it, do spells and chants to call it into our lives, have faith that it will arrive. But ultimately—and here's where surrender comes in—it's only when we allow ourselves to float in the great sea of life, giving up all control, trusting it will hold us up, that love will arrive. It may come just when you want it, or so long after you were dying to get it that you've given up and aren't even sure you want it anymore. You just never know.

Like a Christmas present, it may be exactly the thing you hoped you'd find under the tree—or something you never imagined or dreamed of. The paradox is that, if it is love, you accept it in whatever form it arrives—even if it isn't precisely what you asked for.

For no matter how love arrives, no matter how well or imperfectly, the amazingly wonderful thing is that when it does arrive, it takes over. You can do nothing but jump for joy and throw up your arms and shout, "I'm in love! Can you believe it? I've finally found the love of my life!"

Do Everything and Do Nothing

Because love is paradoxical, you'll never find a mate unless you stop looking, and at the same time, you need to ask, want, hope, prepare, and be in a state of total anticipation for the person of your dreams. You need to change your bed sheets, buy new clothes, and get that great haircut—*and* you need to sit at home listening to Mozart or Peter Gabriel and filing your fingernails. You need to operate with the absolute conviction that love will show up and, at the same time, with the absolute acceptance that you'll be just fine if it doesn't.

That's because you have to be in a state of surrender. When you surrender, you're so open that finally something as out-of-control as love can actually come into your life. If you're too busy taking charge, you'll only get love of the size, shape, and contents you can imagine. Conversely, if you do nothing at all and hide out in your bedroom, you won't be available to the possibility of love. You have to do both.

When we embrace the paradox of love, we're trusting on all levels. We're trusting on the spiritual level that the forces of the universe will be on our side. We're also giving up control on the emotional level—where we want, desire, long for, and pout—and on the mental level—where we plan, scheme, and analyze. Instead of saying, "I'm so smart, I've figured out exactly what kind of person would be perfect for me, and that person had better show up next week;" you say, "I'm going to release my hold on the outcome. I'm letting go of what I want; what my parents would want for me in a mate; what the dating service statistics say my possibilities are. Instead, I'm going to flow. I'm not going to go *with* the flow, I myself am going to *become* the flow; and on this winding river of fluid movement, the love of my life can come in."

Know It Will Take Longer Than You Think, and It Can Happen at Any Moment

Another paradox has to do with timing. Love will come late or soon, long after you hoped, much quicker than you imagined. It will feel like it's faster than a race horse, slower than molasses in January. You need to be ready to take it either way, welcome it whenever it comes. Since you don't really know when it's going to show up—no matter how carefully you lay your plans—you can't *expect*, but you should prepare. You've got to put the sugar-water out in the magic hummingbird feeder, even though you can't be sure that the hummingbird's going to show up tomorrow morning, or even in your lifetime.

It's this combination of preparation and surrender that is the spiritual matrix in which love can arrive. Being able to inhabit this paradox comfortably is really a spiritual undertaking. That's because after you've put forth such a magnificent effort—that Club Med vacation, all those blind dates, those Chamber of Commerce mixers, prayer, rituals, weeping, and gnashing of teeth—it's really difficult to say, "Well, now that I've done all that, I'm going to let go." Only your spirit can do that.

Just the same, you *have to* let go. That's the surrender. And only in the letting go will anyone appear. Only in forgetting to watch the clock will the soup cook, the eggs boil, and the love of your life show up. In the case of my friend who met the love of her life only six months after her divorce, she *had* given up, surrendered to whatever would happen (even if it were nothing). As a consequence, she was totally available for the man who came along, an artist with a gentle spirit, the kind of man she never before would have thought of as a possible match for her.

The Pearl of Great Price

Love *is* a gratuitous gift of the gods, but it doesn't come for free. Indeed, the value of any love is exactly commensurate to what you have paid for it. When you fall in love and are wild with delight, you've arrived at that place because of everything you've already chosen- and everything you've surrendered up to that point in your life.

As you've seen as you worked your way through this book, you have paid for the love you are seeking now through all the teachings, lessons, and experiences of every relationship that's preceded this one—whether that was the puppy love of your childhood, the first love of adolescence, a long-term love that never quite gave you satisfaction, or the precious love that was snatched untimely from you.

Indeed, as we've seen, the love you need now is in some profound sense the culmination of all the loves you've already lived, the great ones and the sweet ones, the romantic island interludes, the long, demanding commitments—whether they filled you up or emptied you out.

You are now standing here available to love *because* of all the times your heart has been broken, because of all the good fights you've had in the past, because of the tedious conversations you went through in which you learned to speak your feelings, because of all the difficult choices you've made in your life—to work and play, to grow, to change, to give up. Everything you've done and been through has brought you to the place where you can be open, willing, receptive, and daring enough to fall in love at this moment.

No matter what it is, there's always a price to pay for a love, and the price reveals its true value. It's beautiful in a way, because when you actually see what you've paid for the love that comes into your life, you suddenly see how incredibly precious it is. When you're falling in love, you're often so exhilarated by the onslaught of positive feelings that you're not thinking of all you've done and been through to get there. You're not saying, "Oh, my goodness, look how I've had to grow and change in order to be able to love this person; look at all the classes I've taken, relationships I've been through, behaviors I've changed." You're in love, the price is invisible at the moment, but to see the true value of your love, it's also important to remember that everything you've already done has led you to this moment.

There's also an immediate price to pay. Finding the love of your life may mean, for example, saying to your ten other boyfriends, "I need to say good-bye to you now," or to your children, "I'm reading you stories early tonight because I have a date," or, "I'll be away for the weekend." It may mean saying to your parents, "I'm moving across the country because the woman I can't live without has just showed up in my life." Love could ask that you give up your job, house, pet, or professional colleagues. It may mean separating yourself from friends who may not approve of the connection you've made, or from your parents who refuse their support of your choice.

A man met a beautiful woman on a bus going from the airport into the city of Paris. They sat together in the front seat talking quietly, exchanging stories and then, finally, because they felt a special connection, also their names and the telephone numbers of where they each would be staying in Paris. After some time, the bus arrived at the man's destination, and, disembarking, he set his satchel down on the sidewalk, waved, and then blew a kiss to the woman who had so captivated him. At that very moment a thief ran off into the inky night with his satchel, leaving him empty handed on the sidewalk, without even so much as the scrap of paper on which he'd written the woman's telephone number.

Three days passed, and naturally the woman hadn't heard from him. She thought perhaps he had forgotten her or that their meeting hadn't been as special as she imagined. But since she'd felt a touching connection, and he had also given her his telephone number, the woman decided, somewhat shyly, to step over her own sense of etiquette and call him. He was delighted she called and told her how his valise with six pairs of glasses, his camera, his checkbook, his return airplane ticket, her phone number, and all his clothes except what he was wearing, had been stolen. Finally he said, "You must be the love of my life, because look how much I've paid for you."

For most of us, what we pay for a given relationship won't be so graphically visible or romantically enchanting, but in one form or another we do all pay for the loves that come into our lives. We pay through leaving the partners who didn't suit us and going through the anguish of ending a relationship; by giving up addictions and changing patterns of health; by moving out of our parents' house against their wishes in order to have some privacy to entertain a date; or by crying our eyes out in solitude for god-knows-how-many years. Whatever you've done in the process of getting yourself ready for love, that is the price you have paid.

As you look toward the arrival of a new love, be aware that there will also be a price this time. As you find yourself contemplating giving up your house or apartment, bearing the wrath of your children as they uncomfortably become familiar with your new mate, or the disapproval of your parents or siblings, realize that, along with being uncomfortable and even perhaps upsetting, these things also tell you how much you treasure the love you are choosing.

Love Just Happens, Love Never Just Happens

Another of the grand paradoxes of love is that love just happens—the person you couldn't imagine just one day shows up—and at the same time, love never just happens. Love doesn't "just happen," because in the background of every successful relationship is a story of how intention and opportunity converged in time.

There are always a whole set of circumstances, chance occurrences over which lovers have no control, which set love in motion. You go to the party because your flight was canceled, and *she* is there just for that one day because she's in town to visit her sister. You drive three hours to be on the panel you thought would be a crashing bore in order to meet the man of your dreams, who flew across the country to be there. Or you get divorced, and in the halls of divorce court, bump into the lawyer who, two years later, will become your second husband.

Love is like a string of pearls, a series of experiences, which strung together one by one, become the exquisite whole with which you can adorn yourself. In this sense, love never "just happens." Every event or person leads to the next, and the whole cannot exist without the parts.

To get a sense of this, it's useful to trace the family tree of your relationships. In my own life, for example, when I look at my dear ones and friends and ask myself, how did this person come into my life, there's always an interesting story, sometimes many "generations" of connection. My friend Paul, for example, was introduced to me by my friend Sherry who worked at a magazine with him. He'd read one of my books and started talking to her about it; they became friends. Three years later my friend Suzanne had a birthday party for her friend Jane and invited me. Unbeknownst to me, Suzanne had known Sherry for 12 years, and so invited Sherry to Jane's party. Sherry didn't want to come alone, so she invited Paul. We finally met. He knew my friend, Hal, the photographer, who'd worked with him on an article once. So instantly we had not only two friends in common, but several shared interests on which to build our own friendship.

We all have similar stories. Every experience links to another. Your beloved may come to you through someone who knows you or through a class you both take. Or you'll ride the same bus with her for five years and finally have a conversation. Or perhaps he'll be the guy who's walked down your hall to the water cooler 56 afternoons in a row and you finally make a little joke he enjoys. Or maybe she stumbles into you at a phone booth in the airport, hires you to do some work, or is your little brother's best friend.

I have a friend who went to a party years ago and saw a very dashing man across the room. Involved with someone else at the time, she just noted in passing that he was the most attractive man she'd seen in years. Three years later, her relationship over, much to her surprise, she was introduced to this same man one day at her office. He'd just joined the mortgage firm next door and was being introduced to the people in the other offices. "I couldn't believe it was him," she said. "When I mentioned that I'd seen him before, at that party," he said, 'I was so involved with someone else, I don't recall seeing you.'" When I winced, he added, 'don't worry, it was a terrible involvement, the most horrible relationship of my whole life.'" Suddenly finding themselves in proximity, and both available, they struck up a passionate acquaintance, and have now been together for two years.

That's how love "just happens" and never "just happens." It's part of the elaborate, spiralling lineage of people and circumstances that constantly criss-cross our lives. The person who will step into your life to love you has been coming to you from just as far, through just as many terrible and wonderful experiences, as you have—through swamps and thickets, wearing slippers and combat boots, assisted by angels. When the moment of your convergence arrives, it may *seem* like he or she appeared out of nowhere, but in fact she came to you from everywhere; he came to you through everything. Surrendering to this truth is trusting in its reality and being willing to wait for its happy occurrence.

Love Is a Million Miles Away and Right in Front of You

Love is the unexpected, expected guest, the person you both wait for and give up on at the same time. Love is the woman who's been your dearest friend for a dozen years, who was so much a part of the fabric of your life that you never could see her as a woman to actually fall in love with. Love is the man who came to you with his problems about his breakup— you were just trying to be helpful and then you fell in love in the process. Love is the invited, uninvited guest: arriving because you've been asking for love forever, and arriving too late because, ditto.

Love is a miracle, an accident, a wild hair of a chance and a surefire inevitability all rolled into one. It's so easy and so impossible that when you do fall in love, it seems like the easiest thing in the world—you wonder why you didn't do it a long time ago. But when you're waiting to fall in love, it seems like it's the only thing in the world that will never happen to you.

Don't let the paradoxes scare—or confuse—you. They're there like the tricks of a wonderful cosmic sense of humor, to remind you that you really aren't in charge. But if you have faith, intention, and trust—and if you really do surren- der—love magically *will* show up.

Letting go, giving in, and laughing about all the purely mystifying paradoxes love embodies, are some of the best things you can do to bring love into your life. Remember, love is looking for you just as much as you are looking for it. The person who will love you is longing for you just as much as you are longing for him or her. All you have to do is surrender.

10. *Let* Go of Preconceptions

Here you are, at the emotional embarkation point, ready to board the bus, train, plane, or hot air balloon that will carry you to the love of your dreams, most likely loaded with preconceptions about just what kind of person your true love is going to turn out to be. That's wonderful. You've focused your intention and you've identified some preferences. Indeed, in the earlier chapters of this book, I even helped and encouraged you to formulate some of those ideas. Now, in this chapter, I'm going to ask you to let them all go and take a free-fall into love.

Letting go of your preconceptions is where you'll encounter one of the truly amazing paradoxes of love. On the one hand, as I've been saying all along, you need to be focused, specific, and daring, to figure out and ask for exactly what you want. On the other hand, you need to surrender all that, be willing to throw out all your expectations when love in its surprising, unexpected form comes along to blow your socks off. Love has a mind and a heart of its own; and it is only when you surrender your mountain of preconceptions that love can become the gift that it is.

A story to illuminate: Stephanie was a hardworking divorcee who'd come out of a terrible ten-year marriage and was single-handedly raising two children. A paralegal, she came home from work every day, lugging bags of groceries up the stairs to her second-floor apartment. Week after week, she would dutifully make dinner for her kids, read them stories, put them to bed, and do a little of what she liked most to do for herself—spend the evening reading and writing.

One day when Stephanie came home, carrying two bags of groceries, she ran into a handsome young man walking up the opposite set of stairs who offered to carry her bags. Declining his assistance, she later thought, "What a kind man! Wouldn't it be wonderful if I could find somebody like him who was ten years older? He seems so good natured and genuine. Too bad he's so young."

Months went by, and she kept noticing him. One day when she found herself saying again, "I wish I could find a guy like him who's my age," a little voice inside her said, to her great shock and surprise, "I don't want somebody just like him. I want *him*." At that precise moment, she dropped her preconception that the man she would fall in love with would have to be her age, and decided that the next time she saw him, she'd say hello. That was the first of many hellos. They did indeed fall in love and have now been happily married for fifteen years.

Preconceptions are like barnacles that have been on the bottom of a boat for a couple of years. They're nothing fatal; they just have to be scraped off. We all have preconceptions of the ideal mate. Under duress, we may surrender some of them, scrape off a layer or two, but one preconception is often replaced by others, which, in turn, must also be surrendered.

Whoever your true love turns out to be, you will be asked continually to let go of how you thought he or she would be, in order to receive how they actually are. We may think we can define—or even divine—our perfect mate, but the fates have another version in store. As with the woman who thought she was too old for the man on the stairs, you need to abandon all preconceptions and allow fate to take its surprising course.

When I talk about letting go of your preconceptions, I'm not referring to the S.Q.N., which is the thing you truly do need in a relationship. I'm referring to the whole lot of preferences and attributes (like all the ones you put on your wish list), as well as the vast variety of hopes, dreams, and expectations you hold in your unconscious and discover to be incorrect only when the person who doesn't meet your preconceptions is standing right in front of you.

I've always enjoyed listening to disc jockeys, because I'm enchanted by their voices. But on the several occasions when I've met the person behind the voice, I've always been surprised. It's only then that I realize I've invented an entire person to go along with the voice, and I've always had the feeling when the real disc jockey actually materialized, "Now what I am going to do with the person I created in my mind?"

This is an example of how, without our even knowing it, there are certain stimuli that cause us to create misconceptions about people. We may hear a given fact about a person—he's a millionaire or she's a wonderful mother—and then build an entire universe around this single fact. The minute we hear these highly charged bits of information, we can either dismiss them out of prejudice, or build a whole fantasy around them: "He's a millionaire so he certainly couldn't be a man with feelings, and I wouldn't want to get to know him," or "He's a millionaire so I'm sure he's perfect in every other aspect." "She's a wonderful mother so she'll love me well, too," or "She's a wonderful mother so she probably won't have time for me." To the one fact we know, we attach a far-ranging array of our prejudices, hopes, and dreams.

When it comes to love, we each have a whole raft of these preconceptions, some of which we may be aware of and some of which, like the radio announcer, remain completely invisible until we have a chance to check them out in the clear light of reality. For example, when the man you're dating tells you he has four dogs that sleep on the floor beside his bed, and you're somebody who likes to sleep on a white eyelet, poof-pillow boudoir duvet, your preconception that this person will be inappropriate for you might turn on its bright lights and start roaring down the highway. "A relationship with this person could never work out," you might say, discovering your antipathy toward a pack of dogs. The truth is, perhaps this man isn't the one for you, but are you going to let a few dogs stand in the way of discovering if this is true love?

We all create categories in our minds of acceptable and unacceptable traits, and then apply these generalizations to a particular individual. We tend to use these preconceptions as reasons to dismiss someone, especially if we've had a failed relationship with a person who shares this same "contaminated" category. We think we can prevent the bad thing from happening again by eliminating the "tainted" categories. For example: His mother lives in the same town so I'd have to deal with her day and night, and I certainly don't want another mother-in-law. Or, she just got out of law school and has $20,000 in student loans. I'm never going to get involved with a woman who has money problems again.

Such statements, both of which I've heard at least one person say to dismiss someone who might actually have been a very good match, represent a person's desire to control the form and content of the love that will be delivered to them. But love has a life—and a mind—of its own.

Whenever you get too tied to your preconceptions and make absolutes out of them, it's often at this very moment that the cosmos has a surprise for you: the man who shows up at your door may not be the intellectual giant you insisted on having, but he has the biggest heart you've ever run into; after insisting for years that you absolutely would never get involved with someone who's been divorced, you fall in love with a person who's been married three times.

At these times we're called upon to throw out our notions of our "it should be's" and surrender to the mystery.

The person who actually shows up to love us reveals the limitations of our thinking and the whimsy of the universe as it selects a partner for us in the great dating service in the sky. In a sense, our preconceptions represent little bits of ego still waiting to be blown apart by the mystery of love so we can expand into the higher spiritual beings we are here to learn how to be. When we drop our egos and surrender, we get to see the awesome power of love and how our soul is always operating on our behalf.

For example, you may find yourself being resistant to falling in love with someone who smokes, because your mother was a chain-smoker for 43 years and died of lung cancer—a reasonable enough idea. Even though he may be presenting himself as someone who wants to quit smoking, you may have such a resistance to going down this particular arduous road once again—for good reason—that you may shut yourself out of a wonderful relationship.

While many people never change (and we all know about denial), love does perform miraculous transformations. Perhaps being in the presence of someone who actually overcomes an addiction could be the healing of that gaping wound with your mother. By the same token, your being a supportive, loving presence might be just the thing he needs to help him go through the hell of withdrawal and open the door to his new life. Because love on a soul level truly is about evolution—and therefore, miracles—it asks, at times, that we drop our preconceptions so we may be creators and partakers of the transformations that occur.

Wait a minute, I can hear you saying, you've made me do all this work on intention and creating a love wish list and now you want me to throw it all out. What gives?

Believe it or not, there really isn't a contradiction in what I'm saying. Intention is telling the universe you want something. Your wish list is getting specific and focused about what precisely you do want. This is the way you put out your invitation for love. Preconceptions, however, are about you, *not* surrendering and trusting, not letting go of the reins, but deciding, somewhere inside, just how you want your intention and your wish list to be fulfilled. But all that's out of your hands. How your wishes are granted, the way in which your intention is fulfilled—this is in the hands of the gods. That's where surrender comes in. After you've expressed what you need, you have to let go of your preconceptions and let the miracle occur.

What Are Your Preconceptions?

We all create laundry lists of expectations from love. Some of us are just more unreasonable than others. I remember, somewhat amusedly, working with a rather intense young woman who had quite a few emotional difficulties. One day she announced, "I am certainly not going to fall in love with someone who has any emotional baggage. I couldn't put up with that. I'm still trying to get over my father's dropping dead when I was 16 and leaving me with my six brothers and sisters to raise, while my mother was drinking herself to death in the corner."

This young woman obviously had her own share of emotional baggage, yet she was actually operating under the misconception that there was a human being somewhere on the planet who didn't have any, and she was going to wait around until that amazing creature showed up.

We *all* have emotional baggage. Some of us have little overnight bags and some of us have steamer trunks, but we all have our share. Thinking there's actually someone who doesn't have any is sure to bring you a whole lot of lonely nights watching television.

The same is true about other preconceptions. I have a wonderful friend who married a woman with children, had a happy and successful marriage for seven years, then parted company with her in a mutually satisfying way. A few years passed, and then, lo and behold, during a particularly lonely period he started dating a woman who had two children. He was obviously attracted to her on many levels, but every time he talked about her he'd say, "She's really a wonderful woman, but I'm not going to get involved with someone who has children. I've already raised two kids, and I'm never going to do it again."

He was already falling in love with this woman, but his

rule, "I don't want to fall in love with a woman who has children" was causing him to deny the love he was already in. But love was bigger than his preconception, because he is now married to this woman, and in time he discovered that not only does he love her, he also deeply loves her children. This only goes to show that preconceptions are often misconceptions; like rules, they're made to be broken.

Single people looking for love are running around with bags full of these misconceptions; a common one is: "It's not good to marry a widow or widower, especially if they really loved the person who died. How can you step into somebody else's shoes? You either won't fill them—or they'll pinch." The truth is that anybody who really loved somebody once is a person who knows how to love. That kind of person, when the timing is right, makes a wonderful candidate for love.

Another common preconception is that there are certain epochs in our lives that constitute bad timing for falling in love. For example, "You shouldn't fall in love right after you've broken up with somebody." That's certainly a valuable, middle of the road, general-store sort of premise. We all know it's important to do your emotional laundry on an ended relationship before you step into another one, but there are a multitude of exceptions to that rule too. When a relationship ends, particularly if it's been dying a long, slow, gasping death, the person in it may have already gone through the separation, detachment, and growth process during its demise, which might paradoxically make him or her the most perfect candidate for falling in love.

Then there's the "rule" that you shouldn't fall in love for at least a year if you've had your heart broken. I'm reminded of the story of a young woman who happily planned her marriage, and was delightedly in the throes of receiving her wedding gifts, only to be told by her husband-to-be, four days before the wedding, that he'd changed his mind. Once she'd endured this devastating blow, she decided, "That's it! I'm never going to fall in love again. In fact, I'm not even going to date for a year." Instead, she was going to soberly contemplate the disaster that had befallen her, focus on her work, and cry her eyes out, while she sent back all the wedding presents.

But one day, only a few months later, as she was going through her crying-her-eyes-out period, a man who often passed her in the hall at work noticed she was distressed and invited her out to lunch. You can guess the rest of the story. Before she'd so much as managed to send all the wedding gifts back, she was already feeling a deep and tender love for this man, and long before her year of "I'm not even dating anybody" was over, she was engaged to be married. The sequel?—just to make sure this wasn't a ricochet romance—this badly timed first meeting has resulted in a most happy six-year marriage and one baby girl.

Preconceptions stand in your way if you don't bring them to light and have the courage to surrender them. So take a moment now to think about the rules you've created for this person you want to enter your life. Do any of these sound like something you'd say?

- "He just got divorced so he's a bad candidate for marriage. I'm never dating a divorced man again."

- "He's never been married so obviously he can't make a commitment."

- "She's had a struggle with alcoholism in the past so the fact that she's been sober eight years is irrelevant."

- "He had five children with his first wife so obviously he wouldn't want to have any more."

- "He isn't tall enough."

- "She isn't pretty enough."

- "I like a smart man, and he's not smart enough."

- "He doesn't have enough money; I don't want a man who can't spoil me."

- "She doesn't have a good enough job. I don't want a woman I have to support, I want a woman who will share the burden."

Any of these preconceptions may be yours, or you may have your own idiosyncratic list. Whatever yours are, it's important to remember that they're poison arrows to the heart of a promising love. If you're running around with a quiver full of these relationship-killer darts, you're not going to be open to the possibilities of the relationship that may be coming toward you. However, the moment you become aware of them, you automatically start dismantling them—and increasing the potential that love will break through to you.

One final thing about preconceptions—just like any of the other paradoxes about love—they may be appropriate or they may be completely bogus, off-the-wall items that you should toss in the trash can. The things on your check list *are* worth keeping as guidelines. At the same time, be willing to throw them all over if the person whose soul speaks to yours comes along.

Love Will Never Be Perfect

If preconception were the name of an undiscovered continent, perfectionism would be its furthest outpost. Perfectionism is preconceptions to the Nth degree. We all have little—or gigantic—pockets of perfectionism embedded in our love dreams. On one level, this is our imperfect personality's desire to experience perfection somewhere; on another level, it's a kind of stubborn addiction to the fantasy that perfection exists, and we can have our share.

On the higher level, perfectionism is an expression of the longing for that state of purity that is our soul's true condition, that state of beauty and loveliness we recall from the world of the spirit before we took on human form. Our souls, which remember this blissful perfection, say in this life, "I remember that! How can I attain that again? Perhaps if I find the love of my dreams, I'll experience it again." The soul's longing for perfect union is real, and, indeed falling in love, more than any other human experience, allows us a momentary glimpse of this ecstatic state. But we shouldn't expect it on a daily basis from life here on earth, where true perfection is never quite achieved.

While perfectionism, in all its hairy, demanding, unreasonable aspects, may really just be a longing for the divine, in human relationships, it's the tarantula in the ointment. For many of us, love in the form of a person to *actually* love will never exist, because our idea of who that person should be is so far beyond the realm of what is humanly possible that no matter whom we hook up with, he or she is never quite right.

This perfectionistic ideal has been lavishly reinforced by movies, television, and advertising, all of which encourage us to believe that perfection is possible and that we should get every one of our whims satisfied. Compared to the bronzed gods and buffed beauties we see on-screen, a regular garden-variety person, who's got warts and flaws but who might be comfortable and comforting in an everyday sort of way, often looks painfully less than acceptable.

I know a woman who broke up with a kind, generous man because he left wet towels on the bedroom floor, a man who dismissed a fabulous woman after their first date because she chewed her food with her mouth open, and a woman who rejected a wonderful potential mate because he "smelled funny." Possible true loves have bitten the dust over bigger (and lesser) perfectionisms than these: "she had an odd-looking billfold," "He didn't open the car door for me," "He wore brown socks with his tennis shoes." But no matter how reasonable or unreasonable the content of your particular perfectionism may be, if you really do want to fall in love, you'd better be willing to send all your perfectionistic head trips to the guillotine.

On the psychological level, perfectionism, no matter what its particular focus—looks, housekeeping skills, aesthetic awareness, bathroom habits—is the consequence of many things. Sometimes it's a deep inner resistance to falling in love, because one has a great fear of being overwhelmed or abandoned—we talked about the power of these life themes earlier. In other instances, it's just a basic personality characteristic—fussiness, pickiness, or self-indulgence. In still other cases, it may be a temporarily adopted behavior to help you through a time of crisis.

In this regard, I'm thinking of Shelley, a woman in her late 30s, who came to me weeping on many occasions about how frustrated she was that she had no sweetie-pie. As our conversations went on, it became very clear that, without her being consciously aware of it, she'd made a decision to put all her energies into filmmaking, and wasn't going to stop, come hell or high water, until she'd managed to produce a feature film.

The work involved was unbelievable—more than she'd ever imagined. As her project unfolded, and the nature of the commitment it would require gradually revealed itself, she got sadder and sadder about not having a relationship. But interestingly enough, for each person who came along, she found a reason why he wasn't right for her: He was too short; he didn't have enough money; he didn't dress right; his teeth were crooked.

Without acknowledging it, Shelley allowed in only the kind of relationships—brief, catchy, emotionally shallow—that her life could actually accommodate. She really *didn't* want a full-time relationship at that point in her life; she didn't have time. Her pickiness was her way of remaining single. (By the way, years later, her career well-established, Shelley married in her mid-40s and has just adopted a baby—a reminder that there are stages in everyone's life and you really do need to honor where you are at any given time.)

Then there's Ed, a man who has a gallery of past girlfriends that would make the Miss America Pageant look like the Mummers Parade. Ed's exes are the most extraordinary group of women one can imagine—beautiful, talented, powerful, kind. Through a series of odd circumstances, six of them got together one night at a party. They had a wonderful time getting to know one another, and their consensus was that a) Ed was a fool, and b) Ed really had great taste in women.

Somewhere along the line, in every single relationship,

for one little reason or another, Ed decided that each of them had an attribute he really couldn't stand. Each of the six told why Ed had found her unacceptable. One didn't like mountain bikes; another was afraid of flying; still another had a career he decided was too demanding. One wanted children while he didn't, and the last was crossed off because she didn't have quite the right color hair. They all agreed that, could he have chosen any one of them, he probably would have been happy. Not only that, but there wasn't a one who said she wouldn't have been happy to have married him.

What this hard-to-get rogue was demonstrating in his penchant for perfectionism is that the p-word can make all acceptable candidates somehow, at the last minute, totally unacceptable. Perfectionism is so perfectionistic that it's perfectly invincible. That's why, if you really want a person by your side and in your bed, you'll have to surrender your need for perfection.

Pack Up Your Pickiness

We all have private, little preferences—we'd prefer a man with good manners, a woman who doesn't run around with three-inch wide runs in her stockings—but we need to be careful that these don't become manifestations of perfectionism gone wild. Yes, all these preferences do refer to things that are actually irritating, things we won't adapt to easily and may have to struggle with, but they shouldn't be the core issue when you're falling in love. Focusing on them turns them into the needle in the haystack. In this case, it's not the needle you can't find in the haystack; it's the needle that gets so big that the haystack is invisible.

Be careful not to be too picky about love. It's here to surprise you; but it will have its limitations. It will be more humble and plain and comfy than the grand romance novel or the Perfect 10 you may have had in mind. It will be bigger than your preconceptions, and even, believe it or not, more perfect for you in some ultimate sense than what you think would be perfect for your perfectionism.

So put away your perfectionist's list of pickinesses. They're not at the level of your S.Q.N., and if you elevate them to that level, they'll become the means whereby you'll always be a loser at love.

Finally, remember that all your picky, little preferences really don't have anything to do with what love is actually about. The minute real love steps through your door—love that opens your heart, touches your soul, and actually alters your consciousness—you will experience a quality of love so far beyond all your perfectionistic principles that they'll all go out the window in the twinkling of an eye.

The truth is, the person who's going to show up one of these days to be the real-life love miracle that you've been waiting for defies all your rules and expectations, perfectionistic and otherwise. Along these lines, I'm always amused by the story of a man I knew years ago. He was so determined to get married by the time he got out of college that he made a list of the 34 attributes he felt necessary in the woman who would be his bride. Then he proceeded, in a very organized fashion, to date each girl on campus to whom he'd been even mildly attracted, to see if she met his requirements.

Finally, after much dating, he found a girl who matched perfectly every single item on his list. He promptly proposed; they were married soon after his graduation, and—as he told me years later—he's been completely miserable ever since.

As his sadly humorous story shows, perfectionism is a faulty guideline. For love is a mystery that defies all lists. So when you've found what you think is love, don't ask yourself, has this person hit the 99th percentile on my perfectionist nit pick list. Instead, ask yourself, Do I feel loved? Do I care deeply for this person? For it is only the feeling of loving and being loved that will enable you to build a relationship where the daily, ordinary, and extraordinary happenings of love will continually occur.

11. *Leap* into the Unknown

Now that you've prepared yourself by examining your past, defining what you want now and surrendering to your soul's wisdom, love is waiting to come out of the vast mysterious ethers and greet you—on your doorstep, on a street corner, in the seat beside you on an airplane, in line behind you at a telephone booth, from across the crowded room at a boring business party.

But these happy accidents can only occur when you take a leap into the unknown. This is a gesture in which your faith, intention, and trust all become embodied in an *act* of surrender. The leap of faith is an actual movement—of the body, the spirit, or the emotions—in which you gather all your energies and say, "I'm going to surrender to love through some specific action."

This action could be something as simple as accepting a second date, or as complicated as learning another language. But no matter what it is, it's often surprisingly difficult to take. That's because at precisely the moment love arrives in the form of a person we're tantalized by, at this very same moment a lot of our negative feelings also decide to show up: *It's too good to be true; it's never going to work out; this person isn't right for me.*

It's a paradox of life that beautiful moments can often be accompanied by their difficult counterparts. That's because both sides—good and bad, joy and sorrow, delight and fear—make up the whole of the human experience. For this reason, when we meet a possible someone, we also encounter our doubts. In the moment of feeling our bliss, we also feel our insecurities. We want to live happily ever after, but we also encounter our fear of loss.

I used to love a story called *The Three Sillies* that my mother read to me when I was a little girl. In it, a family was having a beautiful dinner because their daughter's fiance had arrived from the far country. They'd roasted a pig and made a fine pie and were all sitting down at the table to feast, when the father asked the young man to go down to the cellar and bring up another bottle of wine for the celebration. Just as he started down the stairs, the mother began to weep and wail. "Why are you so unhappy?" asked the father. "We're having such a wonderful time." "Well," said the mother, weeping and wailing some more, "I was just thinking about our daughter's new husband and how wonderful it is they're getting married, and now he's going down the stairs to get a bottle of wine, and there's a hatchet hanging over the door to the cellar and I thought, what if he goes down the stairs and stubs his toe on the steps, and the hatchet falls off its hook and cuts off his head, and he dies and she loses him before they ever get married?"

Here is the fairy tale version of the dilemma that we so often find ourselves in: that in every possible fulfillment, there's also the potential for great loss. The young bride-to-be's mother was expressing the deeply buried fear we all share, that when we fall in love we're letting ourselves in not only for love, but also for possible loss. That's why, even as we're enjoying the experience of happiness and delight, we are haunted by doubts and fears.

We may find ourselves saying to the other person, for example, "You're here now, but will you love me forever?" Or, "We've fallen in love, but now you have to go on that fishing trip with the boys, and I'm scared you'll forget me."

Sometimes it's something we say to ourselves: I'm happy now, but when is the bad part going to show up? Or, this is too wonderful to handle so I'm going to put on the brakes and hold myself back, or test you upside, downside, and sideways to see if you really are the man or woman you appear to be.

There are all sorts of ways we test one another in love, particularly at the outset. We spoil holidays, mistreat each other over money by asking for too much, being too stingy, or giving so much that our partner feels beholden. We may bring up old girlfriends or lovers, say we're not really ready for a relationship, or decide to take a solo vacation to see if this new person is really serious enough to stick around. One way or another we check each other out to make sure, as much as we can, that this person isn't going to fail or disappoint us, leave us, or have some terrible flaw that we hadn't been prepared for.

Love is always accompanied by doubts. If you can remember that feelings of uncertainty are a natural counterpart to strong feelings of connection, you can be both strong and graceful with your doubts. When you meet a special person, are feeling terrified, and want to run like hell, there's a spiritual choice you have to make. You can align yourself with your doubts and back off from the relationship. Or you can step over them, put them, as it were, in your back pocket and say, "Yes, here are all the difficult, scary, and absolutely devastating things that could happen now that I'm feeling so deeply connected. Because I'm feeling such joy, I *could* feel the most devastating sorrow if I lost this. But in spite of that sad possibility, I'm not going to let go of this love. In fact, I'm going to hold on to it, cherish it, and enjoy it for every minute it lasts."

This is the big leap of faith, the one that chooses love in the face of possible loss, and represents the triumph of hope over the tyranny of doubt and fear. When we meet a person worthy of our love, this is the one leap we can't avoid making, the leap that is asked of everyone who truly wishes to be in love.

Be Prepared to Take Action

Any leap of faith requires taking action at a critical juncture, knowing that if you don't act, the moment will pass and love may be lost forever. Sometimes, as we've seen, this leap is an internal jump over your resistance, ambivalence, and fear. At other times it expresses itself through some concrete action such as becoming engaged, getting married, or living together.

But sometimes a leap of faith is required that involves a combination of these two. I know a man and woman, Ted and Alice, who lived on opposite sides of the country and met at a tennis camp. Each of them had been divorced and wanting to fall in love for quite a long time. Through wonderful days of tennis matches and conversation, they each began to have inklings that the other was "the one." By the time the week was over, they recognized they were in love.

At that point, they had a choice. Either they could say something vague that would protect their emotional vulnerability —"This has certainly been a lovely interlude; maybe our paths will cross again." Or they could take some definitive action—a leap of faith that would demonstrate that they really were the answer to each other's invocation of love. They chose to be brave. Before they parted, they acknowledged their love and said, "Whatever we do, we're not going to let this incredible love escape us."

Then they went back to their homes on opposite sides of the continent. Within a week, Ted called Alice and said, "I'm asking you to marry me right now, because if we don't take this deep feeling and put it into a commitment, it will dissipate because we live so far away." She agreed, and within three weeks they were married and have since created a life in which they live in each of their houses for part of the year.

While they both acknowledge that from time to time there are logistical difficulties with this arrangement, they look upon it as a challenge well worth going through. Above all, they both believe with absolute conviction that if they hadn't taken a leap of faith at that very moment to "impulsively" get married, the love they now share may well have eluded them forever.

I love "impulsive" love stories because so often they represent the real courage and wild bravado of taking a gamble on love. Amanda and Philip also lived in two cities quite far apart. Amanda, a successful decorator in her mid-50s, was married young and divorced in her early 30s. After raising her children on her own and getting them all through college, she had finally applied her talent to create a beautiful home for herself. She was so delighted with her creation that, as she herself often said, her house had become the man in her life. "It protects me, nurtures me, and delights me. What more could I ask? I don't really need a man in my life."

Then one night, she went to a party and met Philip, who had been divorced for many years. He was an attorney, had spent a great deal of time with his children who were now all grown, and had traveled extensively. He, too, was completely happy with his life and very involved with his career. Yet the minute they saw one another, they realized that they each had been asking for such a love to come into their lives.

They had a brief courtship and after a very few weeks, Philip said to her, "I want you to come and live with me, because my work can't be transplanted, while yours can, and I want to spend the rest of my life with you." Amanda took a leap of faith. Within a week, she put her house on the market. It sold within two weeks, and before a month had passed, she had moved into Philip's house, where she reestablished her career and where, together, they've been living happily for nine years.

As these marvelous stories demonstrate, a leap of faith isn't just a little hop, skip, or jump to the next number on the hopscotch game on the sidewalk; it's a big, scary daring leap, more like a trapeze artist's flying in utter trust through the air, a parachutist's jumping out of an airplane, a mountain climber's hanging on a rope across the cavernous abyss between two mountains. These aren't piddling little half-hearted transactions. They ask that we marshal our energies on every level and say the resounding "yes" that allows us to move from wherever we are into the presence of love.

Of course, such a leap doesn't always mean a circumstantial change. For many people, it means gathering your courage to go through the inevitable hurts and disappointments that lie along the road to a relationship: tidbits of unreadiness, pieces of unfinished business, small scares, big interruptions, and irritating inconveniences that are often the frustrating tests of new love.

For example, you've fallen madly in love, and he says

don't rush him, he still needs a little more time; he wants to marry you, but not now, maybe in six months. Your leap of faith is having the patience to wait and trust, not turn on your heels and run off with somebody else. Or, it's the fifth week of your relationship, but he's had this month-long trip to China planned for two years. You have to have the faith to believe your love will withstand his absence, your pining, and his nasty jet lag when he returns.

Leaps of faith are as various as flowers in a spring garden. They may be leaps of spirit, such as believing that love really does await you. Or they might be emotional leaps, such as believing that he is not going to leave like everyone else did. Or they may be as basic as putting your money where your mouth is—buying that airplane ticket to fly to St. Louis to see her, for example.

My client Mark's story illustrates the further reaches of what such a leap might require. After several ultimately unsuccessful long-term relationships, Mark fell deeply in love with Laura and they had plans to marry. About six months into their relationship, he showed up at my office looking a little grey around the gills and announced that Laura had dropped a bomb on him.

The one other man she'd ever had strong feelings for, who'd been married at the time she knew him, had called her out of the blue, said he'd been divorced for a year, and asked her out a date. She told Mark about it and said, "I know this is terribly scary, but I need to meet with him.

Otherwise for the rest of our lives, I'll never know for sure if I made the right choice." Mark was terrified. All he could see was signs of the imminent demise of the one true love of his life.

Worried sick but taking a leap of faith, Mark suggested that Laura have not one date, but several if needed, so she could really get clear about her feelings. He told her he loved her, that he would wait, but the one thing he asked was that, once having had her encounter, she be ruthlessly honest with him.

It was the most difficult weekend of his life, he told me later, but as he went through it, he could feel his strength rising in the face of his fear. He also saw his willingness to go through this experience as a measure of his love. By the time the weekend was over, he was so peaceful he felt that even if he lost Laura to the other man, what had become of him in the process would be Laura's gift of growth to him. As you might guess, Laura came back from the weekend clear-minded and all the more committed to Mark.

Take the Truth Pledge

A leap of faith can also take the form of revealing your feelings about the experience you're having, moment by moment, as you explore the mystery of a relationship with a new person. For many of us, this emotional risk is the greatest leap we can make. Simply having the courage to say what we're actually feeling is the one thing most of us have never done. Just saying, "I'm so happy to see you" can be, on the emotional plane, a risk of gigantic proportions. So is being willing to ask, "Tell me a secret about yourself," or revealing your vulnerability, "It hurt when you didn't call."

For so many of us, such emotional honesty is very difficult. We've been taught to protect ourselves, to put up a false front to lure the other person in. In this regard, I often suggest to people exploring a new relationship that they take The Truth Pledge: "*I promise I'll tell you exactly what I'm feeling, and I am willing to hear exactly what you're feeling as our experience together unfolds.* What this pledge acknowledges is that you are willing to be together in an ongoing emotional exchange, and that you agree to keep one another abreast of where you are in that experience.

Taking The Truth Pledge is entirely contrary to the high-school coquettish etiquette of "playing hard to get," to say nothing of the grown-up "how to snag a man" mentality. Taking The Truth Pledge means that instead of keeping your cards close to your vest, you lay them on the table.

There's a great deal of trust involved in this. It means you're willing to believe that if you actually tell how you feel as the events of your courtship are unfolding, the person you're starting to get to know will continue to want to discover who you are.

What you will get for taking The Truth Pledge is a genuine experience of two real people, and nothing can do more faster for a budding relationship than starting out on an authentic footing. It sets the stage for a relationship that has emotional authenticity as its hallmark, because it allows you to avoid the superficial exchanges that obscure, rather than reveal, who you and your possible sweetheart really are. So if you want to have a real relationship, start it by taking The Truth Pledge.

It's Time to Leap

It's time now for you to take your own leap of faith, whatever that may be. In your heart, you already know what it is. It may be as dramatic as selling your house like Amanda, or getting married on three weeks' notice like Ted and Alice. Or it could be gathering up your courage to talk to that cute guy who lives around the corner. It may mean holding your breath for a weekend like Mark did, or taking The Truth Pledge and speaking your feelings to the woman you met on the airplane. It may mean trusting your excitement, for once, instead of your logic, or knocking off all your nasty, undermining doubts one by one as they poke up their ugly little heads. Whatever it is, once you do it, you will be closer to receiving the delicious fruits of love.

- In the particular situation you're in right now, what would be your leap of faith? (For example, telling Todd how scared I am this might not work out, being willing to wait till Dan is ready to get married even though I want to right now, or leaving the relationship that's not working to create the opening for someone new.)

Whatever your leap of faith, I encourage you to step out from behind the seemingly insurmountable barriers that are making you reluctant to take it. The beauty of leaping is that you always land somewhere new. At best, you'll be launched into the love of your life. At worst, if this particular relationship doesn't work out, you'll be a person with some newly developed skills, more able to invite love in next time. Either way you can't lose. One way or another, taking a leap of faith will bring love closer to you.

12. *Be* Grateful

Gratefulness is living in a state of great fullness in every dimension. When we inhabit this state, no matter what's going on in our lives, we feel that our hearts are full, our eyes are full of beauty, our ears are full of sounds that enthrall and delight us, and our consciousness is full of a fine awareness of the majesty of life.

If you're reading this book because you don't have someone to love right now, it may well be that you think you don't have a thing to be grateful for. "How can I possibly be thankful when the only thing I want I don't have?" you might ask. "Gratitude! What are you talking about?"

That's because gratitude usually seems like an emotion that comes after the fact of some experience. When someone gives you a beautiful gift, you are subsequently grateful. When you are taken out to a lovely dinner, you are appreciative *afterwards*. But in order to prepare for love, you must live in gratitude as a state of anticipation—not as the consequence of already having received something.

This defies our normal sense of the order of things. But when it comes to love, gratefulness is imperative. That's because gratitude is a magnet. It draws toward itself what is similar to it; it attracts what is resoundingly synchronous with it.

In other words, the joyful, thankful heart attracts a person who is also joyful and thankful. The woman who lives in a state of appreciation of life itself will draw into her circle the man who not only gives thanks for his life, but who will also appreciate her. The man who is thankful even in difficult circumstances will draw in a woman whose similar spirit of gratitude will make his life graceful with ease.

When we're not grateful, we reap the rewards of ingratitude: stinginess, poverty, lack, discomfort, confusion, difficulty. As we express our feelings in these negative modes, people who operate on these same impoverished wavelengths will join us in a chorus of whining and complaining. Difficulties will be drawn to us, because our consciousness is like a picnic ground where these energies can sit down and feast.

Conversely, when we live in a state of gratitude, all that is gracious, beautiful, and full of joy will come to us easily. It's interesting to note how so many of these positive words are full of fullness: beauti*ful*, grate*ful*, wonder*ful*, joy*ful*. When we hold these abundant attitudes, when we live in this state of being, our lives will be filled with what we have already adopted as the attitude of our hearts.

That's why it's important to look at every experience of your life—even the difficult ones—as something to be grateful for, because each has offered a gift or a teaching. So if you've had a great relationship, kick up your heels and say hallelujah, and if you have had difficult relationships, be grateful for all the things they have taught you. Whether you've had a taste of love for ten minutes or 50 years, your heart should throb with thanksgiving for each moment of love you've been given.

Let every event be an instructor in your school of gratitude. For gratitude, more than any other state of consciousness you can adopt, is the attribute that can develop your capacity for love, and your capacity for love is, above all, the thing that will draw love toward you.

Practice the Gratitude Attitude

Just as developing the capacity for love is a practice, so is gratitude. When you enter the practice of gratitude, the things for which you can genuinely feel grateful will start moving toward you more easily and surely. If you really want them, you must recognize them with gratitude as they start moseying in your direction—out of their caves and apartments, their athletic clubs and hotel rooms, their swimming pools and skyscraper lobbies. For you'll notice their magnificent approach only if you're grateful enough to see it.

On the other hand, if you're not practicing gratitude, any person who wants to be embraced by the warmth of true love won't have the courage to approach you. He or she'll say unconsciously, "I'm not sure I want to get to know her because she's such an ingrate I can't even tell if she will be happy when I do finally arrive."

Because thankfulness draws love to us, no matter what's

going on in your life, there really is nothing to do but be thankful. Yet when we're so involved in our longing for love, we often miss the myriad things that already exist for us to embrace in gratitude. Thereby, we unconsciously put a block between ourselves and the love that is seeking us.

It's almost as if the great force that gives us life is saying, "If you can't be grateful for the strawberries and cream, for the hollyhocks and Cheerios, if you can't be grateful for the wild grass and the lilacs, then you're obviously not yet ready to receive something as grand and wonderful as love. Your gratitude machine isn't amped up enough yet; we don't want to blow your circuits by sending a love that will tax your capacity for gratitude beyond what you can handle."

Gratitude is a workout of the soul. It's a state of exercising the spirit to remember without ceasing that joy, thanksgiving, and love are our true spiritual condition and that we are all here in grace. When we remember this, we become worthy contenders in the race for love. For having a real, live human being to love, to share your life with, to talk to, make love with, to watch as the changings of age impart their marks and tender touches on his face, her body—that is the grand experience of life for which we can certainly be grateful. But if you haven't prepared for that in the millions of little thanksgivings that can educate you in the grace of gratitude, then you're a candidate for love's passing you by.

Gratitude is love's food, love's inspiration, love's nurse,

angel, and fairy godmother. Indeed, if you wonder whether gratitude is really an essential part of a loving relationship, try a little experiment with the next person you meet. Try not saying thank you for the beautiful roses, the wonderful meal, for his being the great friend he is, for her understanding the way she does, for support, listening, talking, self-revelation, for sharing. Stop expressing your thanks for a couple of days and you'll be really surprised. When the gifts of love aren't acknowledged, they quickly disappear. Every person and every experience has a certain quality of grace—which, if it isn't reinforced, will gradually wither and fade away.

That's why, whether or not you have exactly the kind of love you'd like, your litany just for being alive should be a constant chorus of gratitude: "Thank you for life, thank you for birth, thank you for all the wonderful, difficult, ever-changing, delightful, and mysterious attributes of my personality that I get to play with, struggle against, and expand into. Thank you for this day, this light, this green field, these mountains, this car, this song, this voice, these eyes, this sense of possibility, this work, this play, these friends, this place to come home to, this pillow to lie down on, this food to eat, this air to breathe, this sky to wake up under time and time again."

Whatever happens in your search for the person of your dreams, be grateful; say thank you. Give thanks and be glad for everything you already have and the things that you long for will start to be yours. The consecration of gratitude will make you a person of such exquisite radiance that the love you desire will be unable to resist you. The love of your life, feeling your great love of life, will come hurrying toward you.

ℒove Readiness Inventory

*I*f you have read this book carefully, you are now aware that there are many aspects to finding your own true love. As you've contemplated your answers to the questions posed throughout the book, you have, in fact, moved yourself through a process of preparation. You now have some information you probably never had before, and know some things about yourself that you never knew before. You've probably already changed—let go of an old emotional wound, claimed some neglected beauty, come to terms with a past relationship—because of reading it. Above all, I hope you've started to believe that there really can be a deep love for you.

This Love Readiness Inventory is designed to show you exactly where you are in the process of being prepared for love. If the previous sets of questions were weekly tests, then this is the semester exam, an opportunity to get an overview of where you really are now.

As you complete it, note what has already been resolved for you as well as those areas that remain as your growing edge. It is here you'll want to concentrate your energies—finishing an emotional healing process, clearing some time, trusting the wisdom of your spirit.

This is not to imply that you can't fall in love until all your emotional and spiritual issues have been resolved. None of us is perfectly prepared, and you don't need to have complete emotional and spiritual resolution in order to fall in love. But it's good to note where you are and what might still be standing in your way. This inventory is a map, a picture of where you are now. I wish you further clarity through it—and a sense of renewed excitement about the possibility of love.

1. Emotional Readiness

Emotional readiness consists of living in the awareness that you are an emotional being and that your feelings are constantly operating, whether you're aware of them or not. It also means that you are willing to bring an ever-continuing awareness of your emotional self to an intimate relationship.

You are emotionally ready if:

- You've identified the main theme of your life and, to some degree, are cognizant of how it operates in your relationships;

- You've done some work of self-healing on the wounds of your childhood so that you're not bringing *all* the unfinished business of your past to this relationship to be healed;

- You have some basic relationship skills such as self-awareness, kindness, and communication (the ability to state your own position about the things that need to be commonly negotiated in a relationship, such as money, sex, children, which restaurant you'd like to eat at, and what movie you'd like to see).

- If you don't have these skills (and you say you want to fall in love), what effort are you willing to put forth toward developing them? Individual counseling, couples therapy, reading books on relationship and/or communication skills?

- Your heart is open; you're willing to trust: yourself, the other person, and love itself.

2. Spiritual Readiness

To be spiritually ready to fall in love means that you've brought yourself to a level of maturity in which an act of surrender is possible for you. You're willing to let go of your personality issues to be a spirit embraced by the force of love. You're ready to willingly and joyfully relinquish your own preconceived definitions of who you are and who the other person should be. You trust that your soul is doing what's best for you, and therefore you can risk falling in love. This spiritual attitude of preparation is a kind of trusting in the good outcome that says, "I'm ready, I'm willing, I'm enthusiastic, I'm optimistic."

You are spiritually ready if you:

- Don't try to control everything. To check this out, ask yourself, "What do I try to control in my life? My possessions? My friends? My timing? My finances? It's appropriate to exercise control in some areas, of course; your finances, for example, and your health. But when you try to control people—"Don't tell me how you feel; I don't want to hear it"; "Don't make me feel that way, I can't stand it," or "Don't feel that way; you shouldn't,"—you're not in the state of surrender that's the hallmark of spiritual preparedness. In general, control of other peoples' feelings, circumstances, choices, and psyches is indicative of a lack of spiritual readiness for a relationship.

- You see each relationship you've had as a gift, even the ones that brought painful lessons or didn't last forever.

- You're willing to surrender to the force of love; you're in a state of acceptance of what *it* has chosen to offer you. To check this out, do you still say things such as: "It's got to come in the next three months"; "It's got to feel this way"; "It's got to do this or that for me"?

- You have the aura about you that says, "Approach me, I'm available," rather than holding an attitude that would require the other person to step over a giant barrier to get to you. To check this out, ask yourself: "Do I feel optimistic or resigned? Excited or depressed? Flirtatious or guarded?"

- If you find these issues of spiritual readiness to be difficult for you, are you willing to choose a prayer or meditation that has your surrender as its focus? For example, "I trust my soul and surrender to its wisdom in bringing me the right love for my life." Gratitude is another healing for broken trust and the inability to surrender. If you'd like to increase your trust, you might try to begin and end each day by giving thanks for at least five things. It's amazing how this small practice in itself can bring you into the state of spiritual readiness.

Honor Where You Are

Wherever you may be in your own emotional and spiritual readiness, honor where you are. For wherever you are at this exact moment is the place that you've arrived as a consequence of all the experiences and people that have impinged on you and nourished you from your birth until now. The moment you're standing in now is a beautiful culmination of all that has already been poured into the great vessel of your life. Everything that has happened to you has prepared you for the person who is ready to love you now, the one who will perfectly accompany and assist you on your journey. So don't despair if you've discovered that you're still afraid to surrender or that you're still wounded over the death of your father; chances are the person you'll fall in love with is just the one who will help you with that issue. Knowing this can allow you not only to trust in love, but also to accept yourself exactly as you are.

As well as assessing your readiness, let this be a moment in which you gather *you* to yourself, into the arms of your own incredible love and acceptance—*you*, the beautiful human being; *you*, the deserving lover; *you*, the exquisitely dearly beloved. For the love with which you love yourself is the truest measure of the love you can receive.

So, wherever you are on this journey to love, whatever has brought you here, may you now receive love's highest gift, a real person to love and enjoy.

A Diagnostic Coda: Is This the One for Me?

Because you've read this book and participated in working through some of your own impediments to love, it's very likely that a wonderful love will now come into your life. But since many of us feel insecure about being able to recognize a real love when it comes along, I'm including some guidelines for evaluating your potential beloved.

The right person, "the one," the love of your life, is the person who, first of all, meets that absolutely inviolate criterion, your *sine qua non* of a relationship. This means that the person you're considering has that one thing, that is absolutely unquestionably necessary for you to have in a relationship without your having to edit, reform, or redesign him or her. Whether that's fabulous intellectual interchange, the emotional communication you've been starving for for years, a powerful sexual connection, or spiritual depth, this wonderful person will embody the very thing you've been waiting for, your relationship S.Q.N.

The Medium of Connection

The right person will not only have your S.Q.N., but you and he or she will also share what I call the Medium of Connection. The medium of connection is the avenue, pathway, or frequency through which you always relate to one another, the channel through which you, as a couple, connect. The person who is right for you—and you will discover this very early on in your relationship—is the one with whom you have some doesn't-even-need-to-be-talked-about-because-it's-so-comfortable way of holding your acquaintance, and vice versa.

For some couples, this is conversation, for others gardening or a love of travel, for still others it's the psychic bond of, without words, just understanding each other. For one couple I know it was a shared focus on their ever-evolving financial plans, which for both of them was a source of endless fascination and also provided the financial security that made them both feel loved.

Having a medium of connection means you have some deep thing you share that can always bring you together, no matter what else may be going on in your relationship. It's your way of feeling—even as your relationship goes through changes—that you're still in love. It's the touchstone of your relationship.

As you're embarking on a new relationship with someone, stop and observe how you're relating to this person. What is your medium of connection? Is it walking on the beach, visiting art galleries, having long, soulful talks? Does this bring you both pleasure and deep satisfaction, and above all, is it making you feel connected? When you hit the rough spots in your budding relationship, and you return to this place together, are you able to feel as if you've "come home" to each other once again?

Identifying your medium of connection may be difficult—if you don't really have one. If you do, it will be instantly visible; but if you don't, this may be the reason your relationship isn't feeling quite satisfactory to you. It also may be that your true medium of connection hasn't revealed itself yet. If that's the case, look at the areas from which it might emerge, and see if nurturing your bond in these areas can result in a deeper feeling of connectedness. If it doesn't, you may not have enough common ground to develop a truly satisfying relationship, and it would be wise for you to move on.

What If There Are Problems?

Sometimes we find the person who is right for us, but initially there are some difficulties. I'm reminded here, of the story of a young woman who fell in love quite quickly and unexpectedly with a man she met at an emotional healing workshop. He was there because, just a few months earlier, his young wife had died. These two were very drawn to each other in the intimacy of the workshop's high level of emotional exchange, and soon both began to realize that they were falling in love. For the man, in particular, this was frightening and shocking, because it was only a few months after the death of his wife, and he felt disloyal and guilty.

When they returned to their homes, the man tried to withdraw from the relationship on the basis of what he thought were his principles. "I can't be falling in love," he kept saying to himself. "This can't be real; I'm grieving. That was just a strange interlude, and I'm going to staunch these feelings right now before they confuse me anymore."

The young woman, on the other hand, was aware that in spite of the unusual circumstances, a deep bond of love was already forming between them. It wasn't just a momentary connection, she knew, but a true love looking for its proper timing. In this instance, rather than taking his word for it, or giving up on the love that had already revealed itself, this young woman quietly stayed in contact and persisted over many months in being available while, on his own, the man completed his grieving process. Finally, he realized that he was ready to love again and even, surprisingly, that in some sense this new relationship had been blessed by his wife who had died. He realized that she wouldn't have wanted him to be miserable and alone, and that the woman he was now falling in love with was someone his wife would have loved and enjoyed.

As this lovely story shows, sometimes you have to be patient, or go through a difficult process even in the falling-in-love stage of love. If the person really is the right one, you will know it and willingly go through these difficulties. This is where your leap of faith comes in.

On the other hand, sometimes there are problems that

just can't be overcome, and it's important to get a sense of how long it's appropriate to "work on" a given relationship. It's true that every new love goes through a molting and initiation period, a time when fantasies are sloughed off and the real core nature of the love is revealed. During this time there are many revisions in your awareness of the person you're loving, and of what's going to actually transpire in the relationship.

Sometimes there are revelations that create disillusionment and show that this isn't the love you imagined it to be. Such a revelation could be the shocking disclosure that she is secretly a drug addict, or that without having communicated it to you, he has six children on the other side of the country for whom he's financially responsible.

Such overwhelming disclosures are often relationship breakers, but when they're revealed, our impulse to "fix it" may come up almost as strongly as our impulse to leave. At this juncture, you must be heartlessly realistic. That is to say, instead of using only your feelings of attachment to evaluate the situation, you must leave your heart out of the decision, and look realistically at what the implications of such a disclosure will be over the duration of a long relationship.

Once you receive such a disclosure, you absolutely must act on the information that's been revealed, whether that means making a commitment to conjoint therapy, joining 12-step programs, or splitting up this very minute. At this point, it might be wise to say, "I'm going to set some pa-rameters on this behavior. I'll give it three months (or six) to show a definitive change or improvement." Or "I'm go-ing to insist that rather than just living with my disillusion-ment—and letting it curdle into resentment—we go to therapy together to see what changes some outside help could gen-erate."

In general, once you've done your realistic assessment, waited through your time line, perhaps gained insight from therapy, and hopefully seen some changes, you will know whether this is a viable relationship. There *are* rites of pas-sage and initiation in any new relationship, junctures at which love can deepen and grow or in which the flaws take over. At this point, you have to search your own heart and see whether this problem can be a focus for mutual growth, or it marks the ending point in your relationship.

Whether or not there are specific painful disclosures in your relationship, there will be little difficulties, tests of faith and patience. As you successfully pass through each one of these tests, moments of growth, plateaus of transfor-mation, you will be drawn deeper into the pleasure—and the real work—of your love. You will begin to recognize that you belong together; that a *we* has been formed.

If you discover yourself starting to grow and change imperceptibly, grandly, beautifully, in ways that astonish and amaze you, this is truly the mark of love upon you. If you notice you're becoming more alive, more self-confident or aware, more receptive, strong, or grounded, more balanced or affectionate—these changes are all the evidence of love. When you experience this early on in a relationship, it's a promise of the further changes that lie in store for you as your relationship develops.

Another mark of a real love is that you find yourself being more *loving*, not only basking in the gifts this person brings to you, but also feeling ignited to offer gifts of your own—praise, encouragement, comfort, admiration, vision, support. Real love makes real lovers out of us, makes us generous, willing, and kind. So if you find, as you're in a particular relationship, that you're becoming more expressive, more noble-minded, less judgmental, chances are that you really have found the person who's exactly right for you.

Whether the changes are in the direction of developing your own character, tying up the loose ends of yourself into a cohesive whole, or enhancing your repertoire of loving behaviors, you will recognize true love by the changes that you make. For the changes you make are the signature of love on the tablet of your soul.

The truth is you will know in your heart of hearts when your true love comes along. For "the one" is the person who will make you feel most absolutely, most genuinely, most happily like yourself. He or she will make you feel loved, loving, lucky, and joyful. There will be a kind of mysterious recognition, a deep incontrovertible sense that you're with the right person. Your body will feel alive and whole, and no matter what the person's flaws or idiosyncracies, you will, day by day and year after year, have an ongoing sense of the intrinsic wonderful all-rightness of it all.

For more than twenty-five years, Daphne Rose Kingma has worked as a psychotherapist whose practice has helped hundreds of couples and individuals understand and improve their relationships.

Dubbed the "Love Doctor" by the San Francisco Chronicle, Daphne has appeared as a relationship expert on nationally broadcast television programs including Oprah!, Sally Jessy Raphael, and The Leeza Gibbons Show. She lives in Santa Barbara, California.

For information on Daphne's lectures
and workshops, please write to her in care of:
CONARI PRESS
2550 Ninth Street, Suite 101
Berkeley, California 94710

or

New Directions
P. O. Box 5244
Santa Barbara, California 93150

To Our Readers

CONARI PRESS publishes books on topics ranging from spirituality, personal growth, and relationships to women's issues, parenting, and social issues. Our mission is to publish quality books that will make a difference in people's lives—how we feel about ourselves and how we relate to one another. We value integrity, compassion, and receptivity, both in the books we publish and in the way we do business.

As a member of the community, we donate our damaged books to nonprofit organizations, dedicate a portion of our proceeds from certain books to charitable causes, and continually look for new ways to use natural resources as wisely as possible.

Our readers are our most important resource, and we value your input, suggestions, and ideas about what you would like to see published. Please feel free to contact us, to request our latest book catalog, or to be added to our mailing list.

CONARI PRESS
2550 Ninth Street, Suite 101
Berkeley, California 94710-2551
800-685-9595   510-649-7175
fax: 510-649-7190   e-mail: conari@conari.com
http://www.conari.com